The black bearded barbarian; the life of George Leslie Mackay of Formosa

Marian Keith

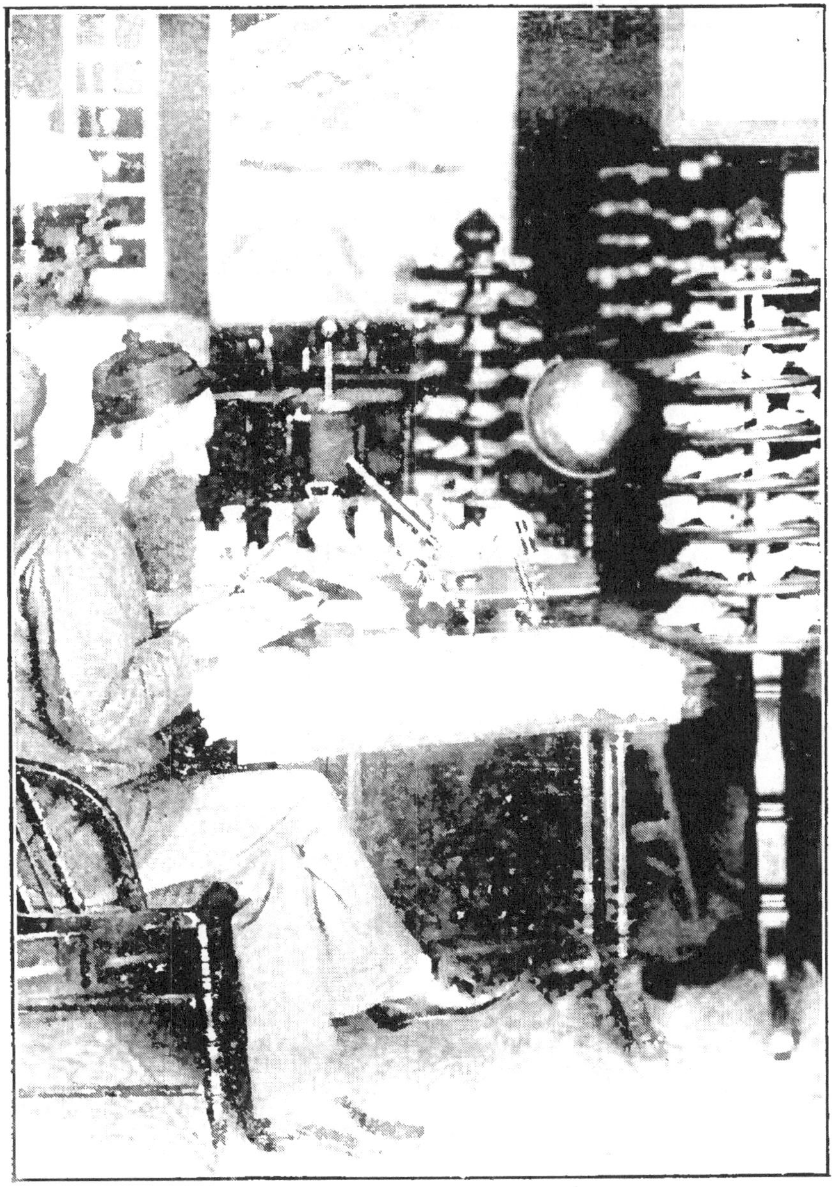

George L. Mackay

"THE BUSIEST MAN IN ALL CHINA"

[*See page* 208]

THE BLACK BEARDED BARBARIAN

THE LIFE OF
GEORGE LESLIE MACKAY
OF FORMOSA

BY
MARIAN KEITH

INTERCHURCH PRESS
NEW YORK

CONTENTS

FOREWORD TO JUBILEE EDITION.

In Israel's early days, the year of jubilee was a glorious celebration. It opened on the day of atonement, and was ushered in at sunrise by a fanfare of trumpets blown by the priests. It brought many gracious laws for the protection of the oppressed, and for the redressing of wrongs. Indeed it was a new start in life for the whole nation. And, best of all, it brought liberty to all Hebrew slaves. With the first sound of the silver trumpets the bondman walked out of the house of his master, a free man.

Just fifty years ago the silver trumpet of the Gospel of Jesus Christ sounded over the lovely flower-decked hills and valleys of North Formosa; just fifty years ago George Leslie Mackay and his first little band of Christian converts met around the table of the Lord for their first communion. And now the Church, scattered all over North Formosa, is celebrating its jubilee.

It is a wonderful story of progress, the record of that fifty years of faithful service, and yet there are many in North Formosa to whom this celebration means nothing. How splendid it would be if the Canadian Church at home were able to say to all that remain in heathen bondage:

"The year of jubilee is come!
Return, ye ransomed sinners, home,"

and see the slaves go free, as they did in the early days in Israel.

And yet that glorious word could be spoken before this jubilee year ends if the Church at home would do her part. When John Geddie, the hero of the New Hebrides, died, it was said of him, "When he came to this Island there were no Christians; when he left it there were no heathen." The "Island Beautiful" is more open to the Gospel than John Geddie's island was. The people are looking toward us with outstretched hands. If every boy and girl, big or little, who reads this story of the "Black Bearded Barbarian" would pray definitely each day for the Island Beautiful, and then plan some real definite work for the missionaries who are toiling there, the year of jubilee would soon be ushered in in reality, and the slaves of heathenism would be set free.

And while we all pray and work at home there will surely be some whose hearts will be moved to carry the silver trumpet to the beautiful land of North Formosa and sound out the glad note of freedom. The missionaries there need our prayers, they need our money, but above all they need helpers: nurses, doctors, teachers, preachers—there are places for them all.

"Lift up your heads, ye gates of brass,
Ye bars of iron yield,
And let the King of Glory pass;
The cross is in the field."

FOREWORD

This is a very little story of a very great man. It contains only a few of the wonderful adventures he met, and the splendid deeds he did. Most of them may never be written. Perhaps they may be lived again in the lives of some of the readers. Who knows?

Even this brief account of Dr. Mackay's life could not have been written had it not been for the help of many kind friends. The Rev. R. P. Mackay, D. D., of Toronto, Canada, who visited Formosa, and met many of the people mentioned in this story, gave me great assistance. Mr. Alexander Mackay, brother of the hero of this book, was very kind in telling many interesting tales of boyhood days in Zorra. My most untiring and painstaking assistant has been the Rev. J. B. Fraser, M. D., of Annan, Ontario, formerly of Formosa. You will find him among the many heroes of this story. To his kind and careful oversight is due much that gives this little book any value as a history. The life of Dr. Mackay in *From Far Formosa,* compiled by Dr. J. A. MacDonald, editor of the *Toronto Globe,* has been my chief source of information. Indeed this story has been taken almost entirely from its pages, and owes Dr. MacDonald much thanks.

And now there is just one more favor it asks, that you who read it may in some measure strive to catch the great spirit of its hero.

MARIAN KEITH.

Toronto, Canada, April 24, 1912.

SPLITTING ROCKS

THE BLACK BEARDED BARBARIAN[1]

CHAPTER I

SPLITTING ROCKS

UP in the stony pasture-field behind the barn the boys had been working all the long afternoon. Nearly all, that is, for, being boys, they had managed to mix a good deal of fun with their labor. But now they were tired of both work and play, and wondered audibly, many times over, why they were not yet called home to supper.

The work really belonged to the Mackay boys, but, like Tom Sawyer, they had made it so attractive that several volunteers had come to their aid. Their father was putting up a new stone house, near the old one down

[1] The name by which George Leslie Mackay was known among the Chinese of north Formosa.

there behind the orchard, and the two youngest of the family had been put at the task of breaking the largest stones in the field.

It meant only to drag some underbrush and wood from the forest skirting the farm, pile them on the stones, set fire to them, and let the heat do the rest. It had been grand sport at first, they all voted, better than playing shinny, and almost as good as going fishing. In fact it was a kind of free picnic, where one could play at Indians all day long. But as the day wore on, the picnic idea had languished, and the stone-breaking grew more and more to resemble hard work.

The warm spring sunset had begun to color the western sky; the meadow-larks had gone to bed, and the stone-breakers were tired and ravenously hungry—as hungry as only wolves or country boys can be. The visitors suggested that they ought to be going home. "Hold on, Danny, just till this one breaks," said the older Mackay boy, as he set a burning stick to a new pile of brush.

"This'll be a dandy, and it's the last, too. They're sure to call us to supper before we've time to do another."

The new fire, roaring and snapping, sending up showers of sparks and filling the air with the sweet odor of burning cedar, proved too alluring to be left. The company squatted on the ground before it, hugging their knees and watching the blue column of smoke go straight up into the colored sky. It suggested a camp-fire in war times, and each boy began to tell what great and daring deeds he intended to perform when he became a man.

Jimmy, one of the visitors, who had been most enthusiastic over the picnic side of the day's work, announced that he was going to be a sailor. He would command a fleet on the high seas, so he would, and capture pirates, and grow fabulously wealthy on prize-money. Danny, who was also a guest, declared his purpose one day to lead a band of rough riders to the Western plains, where he would kill Indians, and escape fearful deaths by the narrowest hairbreadth.

"Mebbe I'm goin' to be Premier of Canada, some day," said one youngster, poking his bare toes as near as he dared to the flames.

There were hoots of derision. This was entirely too tame to be even considered as a career.

"And what are you going to be, G. L.?" inquired the biggest boy of the smallest.

The others looked at the little fellow and laughed. George Mackay was the youngest of the group, and was a small wiry youngster with a pair of flashing eyes lighting up his thin little face. He seemed far too small and insignificant to even think about a career. But for all the difference in their size and age the bigger boys treated little George with a good deal of respect. For, somehow, he never failed to do what he set out to do. He always won at races, he was never anywhere but at the head of his class, he was never known to be afraid of anything in field or forest or school ground, he was the hardest worker at home or at school, and by sheer pluck he managed to do everything that boys bigger and older and stronger could do.

So when Danny asked, "And what are you going to be, G. L.?" though the boys laughed at the small thin little body, they respected the daring spirit it held, and listened for his answer.

"He's goin' to be a giant, and go off with a show," cried one, and they all laughed again.

Little G. L. laughed too, but he did not say what he intended to do when he grew big. Down in his heart he held a far greater ambition than the others dreamed of. It was too great to be told—so great he scarcely knew what it was himself. So he only shook his small head and closed his lips tightly, and the rest forgot him and chattered on.

Away beyond the dark woods, the sunset shone red and gold between the black tree trunks. The little boy gazed at it wonderingly. The sight of those morning and evening glories always stirred his child's soul, and made him long to go away—away, he knew not where—to do great and glorious deeds. The Mackay boys' grandfather had fought at Waterloo, and little George Leslie, the youngest of six, had heard many, many tales of that gallant struggle, and every time they had been told him he had silently resolved that, some day, he too would do just such brave deeds as his grandfather had done.

As the boys talked on, and the little fellow gazed at the sunset and dreamed, the big stone cracked in two, the fire died down, and still there came no welcome call to supper from any of the farmhouses in sight. The Mackay boys had been trained in a fine old-fashioned Canadian home, and did not dream of quitting work until they were summoned. But the visitors were merely visitors, and could go home when they liked. The future admiral of the pirate-killing fleet declared he must go and get supper, or he'd eat the grass, he was so hungry. The coming Premier of Canada and the Indian-slayer agreed with him, and they all jumped the fence, and went whooping away over the soft brown fields toward home.

There was just one big stone left. It was a huge boulder, four feet across.

"We'll never get enough wood to crack that, G. L.," declared his brother. "It just can't be done."

But little George answered just as any one who knew his determination would have expected. In school he astonished his teacher by learning everything at a tremendous rate, but there was one small word he refused to learn—the little word "can't." His bright eyes flashed now, at the sound of it. He jumped upon the big stone, and clenched his fist.

"It's *got* to be broken!" he cried. "I *won't* let it beat me." He leaped down, and away he ran toward the woods. His brother caught his spirit, and ran too. They forgot they were both tired and hungry. They seized a big limb of a fallen tree and dragged it across the field. They chopped it into pieces, and piled it high with plenty of brush, upon the big stone. In a few minutes it was all in a splendid blaze, leaping and crackling, and sending the boys' long shadows far across the field.

The fire grew fiercer and hotter, and suddenly the big boulder cracked in four pieces, as neatly as though it had been slashed by a giant's sword. Little G. L. danced around it, and laughed triumphantly. The next moment, there came the welcome "hoo-hoo" from the house behind the orchard, and away the two scampered down the hill toward home and supper.

When the day's work of the farmhouse had been finished, the Mackay family gathered about the fire, for the spring evening was chilly. George Leslie sat near his mother, his face full of deep thought. It was the hour for family worship, and always at this time he felt most keenly that longing to do something great and glorious. To-night his father read of a Man who was sending out his army to conquer the world. It was only a little army, just twelve men, but they knew their Leader had more power than all the soldiers of the world. And they were not afraid, though he said, "Behold, I send you forth as sheep in the midst of wolves." For he added, "Fear ye not," for he would march before them, and they would be sure of victory.

The little boy listened with all his might. He did everything that way. Surely this was a story of great and glorious deeds, even better than Waterloo, he felt. And there came to his heart a great longing to go out and fight wrong and put down evil as these men had done. He did not know that the longing was the voice of the great King calling his young knight to go out and "Live pure, speak true, right wrong, follow the King."

But there came a day when he did understand, and on that day he was ready to obey.

When bedtime came the boys were asked if they had finished their work, and the story of the last big stone was told. "G. L. would not leave it," the brother explained. The father looked smilingly at little G. L. who still sat, dangling his short legs from his chair, and studying the fire.

He spoke to his wife in Gaelic. "Perhaps the lad will be called to break a great rock some day. The Lord grant he may do it."

The boy looked up wonderingly. He understood Gaelic as well as English, but he did not comprehend his father's words. He had no idea they were prophetic, and that away on the other side of the world, in a land his geography lessons had not yet touched, there stood a great rock, ugly and hard and grim, which he was one day to be called upon to break.

A VOYAGE OF DISCOVERY

CHAPTER II

A VOYAGE OF DISCOVERY

THE steamship *America,* bound for Hongkong, was leaving the dock at San Francisco. All was bustle and noise and stir. Friends called a last farewell from the deck, handkerchiefs waved, many of them wet with tears. The long boom of a gun roared out over the harbor, a bell rang, and the signal was given. Up came the anchor, and slowly and with dignity the great vessel moved out through the Golden Gate into the wide Pacific.

Crowds stood on the deck to get a last glimpse of home and loved ones, and to wave to friends as long as they could be distinguished. There was one young man who stood apart from the crowd, and who did not wave farewell to any one. He had come on board with a couple of men, but they had gone back to the dock, and were lost in the crowd. He seemed entirely alone. He leaned against the deck-railing and gazed intently over the widening strip of tumbling waters to the city on the shore. But he did not see it. Instead, he saw a Canadian farmhouse, a garden and orchard, and gently sloping meadows hedged in by forest. And up behind the barn he saw a stony field, where long ago he and his brother and the neighbor boys had broken the stones for the new house.

His quick movements, his slim, straight figure, and his bright, piercing eyes showed he was the same boy who had broken the big rock in the pasture-field long before. Just the same boy, only bigger, and more man than boy now, for he wore an air of command and his thin keen face bore a beard, a deep black, like his hair. And now he was going away, as he had longed to go, when he was a boy, and ahead of him lay the big frowning rock, which he must either break or be broken upon.

He had learned many things since those days when he had scampered barefoot over the fields, or down the road to school. He had been to college in Toronto, in Princeton, and away over in Edinburgh, in the old homeland where his father and mother were born. And all through his life that call to go and do great deeds for the King had come again and again. He had determined to obey it when he was but a little lad at school. He had encountered many big stones in his way, which he had to break, before he could go on. But the biggest stone of all lay across his path when college was over, and he was ready and anxious to go away as a missionary. The Canada Presbyterian Church* had never yet sent out a missionary to a foreign land, and some of the good old men bade George Mackay stay at home and preach the gospel there. But as usual he conquered. Every one saw he would be a great missionary if he were only given a chance. At last the General Assembly gave its consent, and now, in spite of all stones in the way, here he was, bound for China, and ready to do anything the King commanded.

*As it was then known The Presbyterians in the Maritime Provinces had sent Rev and Mrs John Geddie and others to the New Hebrides and Rev. and Mrs John Morton and others to Trinidad.

Land was beginning to fade away into a gray mist, the November wind was damp and chill, he turned and went down to his stateroom. He sat down on his little steamer trunk, and for the first time the utter loneliness and the uncertainty of this voyage came over him. He took up his Bible and turned to the fly-leaf. There he read the inscription:

Presented to

REV. G. L. MACKAY

First missionary of the Canadian Presbyterian Church to China, by the Foreign Mission Committee, as a parting token of their esteem, when about to leave his native land for the sphere of his future labors among the heathen.

WILLIAM MACLAREN, Convener.

Ottawa, 9th October, 1871.

Matthew xxviii: 18-20. Psalm cxxi.

It was a moment of severe trial to the young soldier. But he turned to the Psalm marked on the fly-leaf of his Bible, and he read it again and again.

"My help cometh from the Lord which made heaven and earth." . . .

"The Lord is thy keeper: the Lord is thy shade upon thy right hand."

"The sun shall not smite thee by day, nor the moon by night."

The beautiful words gave him comfort. Homesickness, loneliness, and fears for the future all vanished. He was going out to an unknown land where dangers and perhaps death awaited him, but the Lord would be his keeper and nothing could harm him.

Twenty-six days on the Pacific! And a stormy voyage it was, for the Pacific does not always live up to her beautiful name, and she tossed the *America* about in a shocking manner. But the voyage did not seem long to George Mackay. There were other missionaries on board with whom he had become acquainted, and he had long delightful talks with them and they taught him many things about his new work. He was the same busy G. L. he had been when a boy;

always working, working, and he did not waste a moment on the voyage. There was a fine library on the ship and he studied the books on China until he knew more about the religion of that country than did many of the Chinese themselves.

One day, as he was poring over a Chinese history, some one called him hastily to come on deck. He threw down his book and ran up-stairs. The whole ship was in a joyous commotion. His friend pointed toward the horizon, and away off there against the sky stood the top of a snow-capped peak—Fujiyama—the majestic, sacred mountain of Japan!

It was a welcome sight, after the long ocean voyage, and the hours they lay in Yokahama harbor were full of enjoyment. Every sight was thrilling and strange to young Mackay's Western eyes. The harbor fairly swarmed with noisy, shouting, chattering Japanese boatmen. He wondered why they seemed so familiar, until it suddenly dawned on him that their queer rice-straw coats made them look like a swarm of

Robinson Crusoes who had just been rescued from their islands.

When he landed he found things still funnier. The streets were noisier than the harbor. Through them rolled large heavy wooden carts, pulled and pushed by men, with much grunting and groaning. Past him whirled what looked like overgrown baby carriages, also pulled by men, and each containing a big grown-up human baby. It was all so pretty too, and so enchanting that the young missionary would fain have remained there. But China was still farther on, so when the *America* again set sail, he was on board.

Away they sailed farther and farther east, or was it west? He often asked himself that question in some amusement as they approached the coast of China. They entered a long winding channel and steamed this way and that until one day they sailed into a fine broad harbor with a magnificent city rising far up the steep sides of a hill. It was an Oriental city, and therefore strange to the young traveler. But for all that there seemed something familiar in the fine European buildings that lined the streets, and something still more homelike in that which floated high above them—something that brought a thrill to the heart of the young Canadian—the red-crossed banner of Britain!

It was Hongkong, the great British port of the East, and here he decided to land. No sooner had the travelers touched the dock, than they were surrounded by a yelling, jostling crowd of Chinese coolies, all shouting in an outlandish gibberish for the privilege of carrying the Barbarians' baggage. A group gathered round Mackay, and in their eagerness began hammering each other with bamboo poles. He was well-nigh bewildered, when above the din sounded the welcome music of an English voice.

"Are you Mackay from Canada?"

He whirled round joyfully. It was Dr. E. J. Eitel, a missionary from England. He had been told that the young Canadian would arrive on the *America* and was there to welcome him.

Although the Canadian Presbyterian Church had as yet sent out no missionaries to a foreign land, the Presbyterian Church of England had many scattered over China. They were all hoping that the new recruit would join them, and invited him to visit different mission stations, and see where he would like to settle.

So he remained that night in Hongkong, as Dr. Eitel's guest, and the next morning he took a steamer for Canton. Here he was met on the pier by an old fellow student of Princeton University, and the two old college friends had a grand reunion. He returned to Hongkong shortly, and next visited Swatow. As they sailed into the harbor, he noticed two Englishmen rowing out toward them in a sampan.[1] No sooner had the ship's ladder been lowered, than the two sprang out of their boat and clambered quickly on deck.

To Mackay's amazement, one of them

[1] A Chinese boat from twelve to fifteen feet long, covered with a house.

called out, "Is Mackay of Canada on board?"

"Mackay of Canada," sprang forward delighted, and found his two new friends to be Mr. Hobson of the Chinese imperial customs, and Dr. Thompson of the English Presbyterian mission in Swatow.

The missionaries here gave the stranger a warm welcome. At every place he had visited there had awaited him a cordial invitation to stay and work. And now at Swatow he was urged to settle down and help them. There was plenty to be done, and they would be delighted to have his help.

But for some reason, Mackay scarcely knew why himself, he wanted to see another place.

Away off the southeastern coast of China lies a large island called Formosa. It is separated from the mainland by a body of water called the Formosa Channel. This is in some places eighty miles wide, in others almost two hundred. Mackay had often heard of Formosa even before coming to China, and knew it was famed for its beauty.

Even its name shows this. Long, long years before, some navigators from Portugal sailed to this beautiful island. They had stood on the deck of their ship as they approached it, and were amazed at its loveliness. They saw lofty green mountains piercing the clouds. They saw silvery cascades tumbling down their sides, flashing in the sunlight, and, below, terraced plains sloping down to the sea, covered with waving bamboo or with little water-covered rice-fields. It was all so delightful that no wonder they cried,

"Illha Formosa! Illha Formosa!"

"Beautiful Isle! Beautiful Isle."

Since that day the "Beautiful Isle," perhaps the most charming in all the world, has been called Formosa.

And, somehow, Mackay longed to see this "Beautiful Isle" before he decided where he was going to preach the gospel. And so when the kind friends at Swatow said, "Stay and work with us," he always answered, "I must first see Formosa."

So, one day, he sailed away from the

mainland toward the Beautiful Isle. He landed at Takow in the south of the island, just about Christmas-time. But Formosa was green, the weather was hot, and he could scarcely believe that, at home in Oxford county, Ontario, they were flying over the snow to the music of sleigh-bells. On New Year's day he met a missionary of this south Formosa field, named Dr. Ritchie. He belonged to the Presbyterian Church of England, which had a fine mission there. For nearly a month Mackay visited with him and studied the language.

And while he visited and worked there the missionaries told him of the northern part of the island. No person was there to tell all those crowded cities of Jesus Christ and His love. It would be lonely for him there, it would be terribly hard work, but it would be a grand thing to lay the foundations, to be the first to tell those people the "good news," the young missionary thought. And, one day, he looked up from the Chinese book he was studying and said to Dr. Ritchie:

"I have decided to settle in north Formosa."

And Dr. Ritchie's quick answer was:

"God bless you, Mackay."

As soon as the decision was made, another missionary, Dr. Dickson, who was with Mr. Ritchie, decided to go to north Formosa with the young man, and show him over the ground. So, early in the month of March in the year 1872, the three men set off by steamship to sail for Tamsui, a port in north Formosa. They were two days making the voyage, and a tropical storm pitched the small vessel hither and thither, so that they were very much relieved when they sailed up to the mouth of the Tamsui river.

It was low tide and a bare sand-bar stretched across the mouth of the harbor, so the anchor was dropped, and they waited until the tide should cover the bar, and allow them to sail in.

This wait gave the travelers a fine opportunity to see the country. The view from this harbor of the "Beautiful Island" was an enchanting one. Before them, toward the east, rose tier upon tier of magnificent mountains, stretching north and south. Down their sloping sides tumbled sparkling cascades and here and there patches of bright green showed where there were tea plantations. Farther down were stretches of grass and groves of lovely feathery bamboo. And between these groves stretched what seemed to be little silvery lakes, with the reflection of the great mountains in them. They were really the famous rice-fields of Formosa, at this time of the year all under water. There were no fences round their little lake-fields. They were of all shapes and sizes, and were divided from each other by little green fringed dykes or walls. Each row of fields was lower than the last until they came right down to the sea-level, and all lay blue and smiling in the blazing sunlight.

As the young missionary stood spellbound, gazing over the lovely, fairylike scene, Mr. Ritchie touched his arm.

"This is your parish, Mackay," he whispered smilingly.

And then for the first time since he had started on his long, long journey, the young missionary felt his spirit at peace. The restlessness that had driven him on from one Chinese port to another was gone. This was indeed *his* parish.

Suddenly out swung a signal; the tide had risen. Up came the anchor, and away they glided over the now submerged sand-bar into the harbor.

A nearer view showed greater charms in the Beautiful Isle. On the south, at their right, lay the great Quan Yin mountain, towering seventeen hundred feet above them, clothed in tall grass and groves of bamboo, banyan, and fir trees of every conceivable shade of green. Nestling at its feet were little villages almost buried in trees. Slowly the ship drifted along, passing, here a queer fishing village close to the sandy shore, yonder a light-house, there a battered Chinese fort rising from the top of a hill.

And now Tamsui came in sight—the new home of the young missionary. It seemed to him that it was the prettiest and the dirtiest place he had ever seen. The town lay along the bank of the river at the foot of a hill. This bluff rose abruptly behind it to a height of two hundred feet. On its face stood a queer-looking building. It was red in color, solid and weather worn, and above it floated the grand old flag of Britain.

"That's an old Dutch fort," explained Mr. Ritchie, "left there since they were in the island. It is the British consulate now. There, next to it, is the consul's residence."

It was a handsome house, just below the fort, and surrounded by lovely gardens. But down beneath it, on the shore, was the most interesting place to the newcomer, the town of Tamsui proper, or Ho Be, as the Chinese called it. The foreigners landed and made their way up the street. To the two from south Formosa, Tamsui was like every other small Chinese town, but Mackay had not yet become accustomed to the strange sights and sounds and stranger smells, and his bright eyes were keen with interest.

The main thoroughfare wound this way and that, only seven or eight feet wide at its best. It was filled with noisy crowds of men who acted as if they were on the verge of a terrible fight. But the older missionaries knew that they were merely acting as Chinese crowds always do. On each side were shops,—tea shops, rice shops, tobacco shops, and many other kinds. And most numerous of all were the shops where opium, one of the greatest curses of Chinese life, was sold. The front wall of each was removed, and the customers stood in the street and dickered with the shopkeeper, while at the top of his harsh voice the latter swore by all the gods in China that he was giving the article away at a terrific loss. Through the crowd pushed hawkers, carrying their wares balanced on poles across their shoulders. Boys with trays of Chinese candies and sugar-cane yelled their wares above the din. The visitors stumbled along over the rough stones of the pavement until they came to the market-place. Foreigners were not such a curiosity in Tamsui as in the inland towns, and not a great deal of notice was taken of them, but occasionally Mackay could hear the now familiar words of contempt —"Ugly barbarian"—"Foreign devil"— from the men that passed them. And one man, pointing to Mackay, shouted "Ho! the black-bearded barbarian!" It was a name the young missionary was destined to hear very frequently. Past opium-dens, barber shops, and drug stores they went and through the noise and bustle and din of the market-place. They knew that the inns, judging by the outside, would be filthy, so Mr. Ritchie suggested, as evening was approaching, that they find some comfortable place to spend the night.

There was a British merchant in Tamsui named Mr. Dodd, whom the missionaries knew. So to him they went, and were given fine quarters in his warehouse. They ate their supper here, from the provisions they had bought in the market, and stretching themselves out on their grass mats they slept soundly.

The next day was Sunday, but the three travelers spent it quietly in the warehouse by the river, studying their Bibles and discussing their proposed trip. They concluded it was best not to provoke the anger of the people against the new missionary by preaching, so they did not go out. To-morrow they would start southward and take Mackay to the bounds of their mission field, and show him the land that was to be "his parish."

ONNOITERING THE TERRITORY

CHAPTER III

RECONNOITERING THE TERRITORY

EARLY Monday morning Mackay peeped out of the big warehouse door at the great calm mountain shrouded in the pale mists of early dawn. The other two travelers were soon astir, and were surprised to find their young companion all ready. They were not yet well enough acquainted with him to know that he could do with less sleep at night than an owl. He was in high spirits and as eager to be off as he had ever been to start for a day's fishing in the old times back in Ontario. And indeed this was just a great fishing expedition he was commencing. For had not One said to him, long long ago when he was but a little boy, "Come follow me, and I will make you to become a fisher of men"? and he had obeyed.

The first task was to go out and buy food

for the journey, and to hire a couple of coolies to carry it and what baggage they must take.

Dr. Dickson went off on this errand, and being well acquainted with Formosan customs and language, soon returned with two Chinese carriers and plenty of food. This last consisted of canned meats, biscuits, coffee, and condensed milk, bought at a store where ships' supplies were kept for sale. There was also some salted water-buffalo meat, a Chinese dish with which the young missionary was destined to become very familiar.

They started out three abreast, Mr. Ritchie's blue serge figure capped by a white helmet on the right, Dr. Dickson on the left in his Scotch tweed, and between them the alert, slim figure of the newcomer, in his suit of Canadian gray. The coolies, with baskets hung to a pole across their shoulders, came ambling along behind.

The three travelers were in the gayest mood. Perhaps it was the clear spring morning air, or the breath of the salt ocean, perhaps it was the intoxicating beauty of mountain and plain and river that surrounded them, or it may have been because they had given their lives in perfect service to the One who is the source of all happiness, but whatever was the cause, they were all like schoolboys off for a holiday. The coolies who trotted in the rear were very much amazed and not a little amused at the actions of these foolish foreign devils, who laughed and joked and seemed in such high spirits for no reason at all.

They swung along the bank of the river until they came to the ferry that was to take them to the other side. They sprang into the boat and were shoved off. Before they reached the other side, at Dr. Dickson's suggestion, they took off their shoes and socks, and stowed them away in the carriers' baskets. When they came to the opposite bank they rolled up their trousers to their knees and sprang out into the shallow water. For a short distance they had the joy of tramping barefoot along the hard gleaming sand of the harbor.

But shoes and stockings had to be resumed, for soon they turned inland, on a path that wound up to the high plain above the river.

"Do you ever use a horse on your travels?" asked young Mackay as they climbed upward.

Mr. Ritchie laughed. "You couldn't get one in north Formosa for love or money. And if you could, he wouldn't be any use."

"Unless he was a second Pegasus, and could soar above the Formosan roads," added Dr. Dickson. "Wait a bit, and you'll understand."

The young missionary waited, and kept his eyes open for the answer. The pathway crossed a grassy plain where groups of queer-looking, mouse-colored animals, half ox, half buffalo, with great spreading horns, strayed about, herded by boys, or lay wallowing in deep pools.

"Water-buffaloes," he said, remembering them as he had seen them in the south.

"The most useful animal on the island," remarked Mr. Ritchie, adding with a laugh, "except perhaps the pig. You'll have a taste of Mr. Buffalo for your dinner, Mackay."

And now they were up on the heights, and the lovely country lay spread out before them. Mackay mentally compared this walk to many he had taken along the country roads of his native land. It was early in March, but as there had been no winter, so there was no spring. It was summer,—warm, radiant summer, like a lovely day in June at home. Dandelions, violets, and many gay flowers that he did not recognize spangled the grassy plain. The skylark high overhead was pouring out its glorious song, just as he had heard it in his student days in Scotland. Here and there were clumps of fir trees that reminded him of Canada, but on the whole the scene was new and wonderful to his Western eyes.

They were now on the first level of the rice-fields. The farms were tiny things, none larger than eight or ten acres. They were divided into queer-shaped little irrigated fields, separated not by fences, but by little low walls of mud. Every farm was under water now, and here and there, wading through his little flooded fields, went the farmer with his plough, drawn by a useful water-buffalo,—the latter apparently quite happy at being allowed to splash about in the mud.

These rice-farms soon became a familiar sight to the newcomer. He liked to see them at all times—when each field was a pretty blue or green lake, later when the water was choked with the fresh green growth, or in harvest days, when the farmers stripped the fields of their grain. Just now they were at their prettiest. Row above row, they went up the mountainside, like a great glass stairs, each row reflecting the green hills and the bamboo groves above. And from each terrace to the one below, the water tumbled in pretty little cascades that sparkled in the sunlight and filled the air with music. For travelers there were only narrow paths between farms, and often only the ridge of the dykes between field and field. As they made their way between the tiny fields, walking along the narrow dykes, and listening to the splashing sound of the water, Mackay understood what Dr. Dickson meant, when he remarked that only a flying horse could be of use on such Formosan cross-country journeys.

Soon the pathway changed once more to the broader public highway. Here there was much traffic, and many travelers carried in sedan-chairs passed them. And many times by the roadside Mackay saw something that reminded him forcibly of why he had come to Formosa—a heathen shrine. The whole countryside seemed dotted with them. And as he watched the worshipers coming and going, and heard the disdainful words from the priests cast at the hated foreigners, he realized that he was face to face with an awful opposing force. It was the great stone of heathenism he had come to break, and the question was, would he be as successful as he had been long ago in the Canadian pasture-field?

The travelers ate their dinner by the roadside under the shade of some fir trees that made Mackay feel at home. They were soon up and off again, and, tired with their long tramp, they arrived at a town called Tiong-lek, and decided to spend the night there. The place was about the size of Tamsui, with between four and five thousand inhabitants, and was quite as dirty and almost as noisy. They walked down the main street with its uneven stone pavement, its open shops, its noisy bargains, and above all its horrible smells. With the exception of an occasional visit from an official, foreigners scarcely ever came to Tiong-lek, and on every side were revilings and threatenings. One yellow-faced youngster picked up a handful of mud and threw it at the hated foreigners; and "Black-bearded barbarian," mingled with their shouts. Mackay's bright eyes took in everything, and he realized more and more the difficulties of the task before him.

They stopped in front of a low one-story building made of sun-dried bricks. This was the Tiong-lek hotel where they were to spend the night. Like most Chinese houses it was composed of a number of buildings arranged in the form of a square with a courtyard in the center. Dr. Dickson asked for lodgings from the slant-eyed proprietor. He looked askance at the foreigners, but concluded that their money was as good as any one else's, and he led them through the deep doorway into the courtyard.

In the center of this yard stood an earthen range, with a fire in it. Several travelers stood about it cooking their rice. It was evidently the hotel dining-room; a dining-room that was open to all too, for chickens clucked and cackled and pigs grunted about the range and made themselves quite at home. The men about the gateway scowled and muttered "Foreign devil," as the three strangers passed them.

They crossed the courtyard and entered their room, or rather stumbled into it, in semi-darkness. Mackay peered about him curiously. He discovered three beds, made of planks and set on brick pillars for legs. Each was covered with a dirty mat woven from grass and reeking with the odor of opium smoke.

A servant came in with something evidently intended for a lamp—a burning pith wick set in a saucer of peanut oil. It gave out only a faint glimmer of light, but enough to enable the young missionary to see something else in the room,—some *things* rather, that ran and skipped and swarmed all over the damp earthen floor and the dirty walls. There were thousands of these brisk little creatures, all leaping about in pleasant anticipation of the good time they would have when the barbarians went to bed. There was no window, and only the one door that opened into the courtyard. An old pig, evidently more friendly to the foreigners than her masters, came waddling toward them followed by her squealing little brood, and flopping down into the mud in the doorway lay there uttering grunts of content.

The evil smells of the room, the stench from the pigs, and the still more dreadful odors wafted from the queer food cooking on the range, made the young traveler's unaccustomed senses revolt. He had a half no-

"You'll be Calling This the Queen's Hotel, before You've Been here Long"

tion that the two older men were putting up a joke on him.

"I suppose you thought it wise to give me a strong dose of all this at the start?" he inquired humorously, holding his nose and glancing from the pigs at the door to the crawlers on the wall.

"A strong dose!" laughed Mr. Ritchie. "Not a bit of it, young man. Wait till you've had some experience of the luxuries of Formosan inns. You'll be calling this the Queen's Hotel, before you've been here long!"

And so indeed it proved later, for George Mackay had yet much to learn of the true character of Chinese inns.

Needless to say he spent a wakeful night, on his hard plank bed, and was up early in the morning. The travelers ate their breakfast in a room where the ducks and hens clattered about under the table and between their legs. Fortunately the food was taken from their own stores, and in spite of the surroundings was quite appetizing.

They started off early, drawing in great

breaths of the pure morning air, relieved to be away from the odors of the "Queen's Hotel." Three hundred feet above them, high against the deep blue of the morning sky, stood Table Hill, and they started on a brisk climb up its side. The sun had not risen, but already the farmers were out in their little water-fields, or working in their tea plantations. The mountain with its groves of bamboo lay reflected in the little mirrors of the rice-fields. A steady climb brought them to the summit, and after a long descent on the other side and a tramp through tea plantations they arrived in the evening at a large city with a high wall around it, the city of Tek-chham. That night in the city inn was so much worse than the one at Tiong-lek that the Canadian was convinced his friends must have reserved the "strong dose" for the second night. There were the same smells, the same sorts of pigs and ducks and hens, the same breeds of lively nightly companions, and each seemed to have gained a fresh force.

It was a relief to be out in the fields again

after the foul odors of the night, and the travelers were off before dawn. The country looked more familiar to Mackay this morning, for they passed through wheat and barley fields. It seemed so strange to wander over a man's farm by a footpath, but it was a Chinese custom to which he soon became accustomed.

The sun was blazing hot, and it was a great relief when they entered the cool shade of a forest. It was a delightful place and George Mackay reveled in its beauty. Ever since he had been able to run about his own home farm in Ontario his eyes had always been wide open to observe anything new. He had studied as much out of doors, all his life, as he had done in college, and now he found this forest a perfect library of new things. Nearly every tree and flower was strange to his Canadian eyes. Here and there, in sheltered valleys, grew the tree-fern, the most beautiful object in the forest, towering away up sometimes to a height of sixty feet, and spreading its stately fronds out to a width of fifteen feet. There was a lovely big plant with purple stem and purple leaves, and when Dr. Dickson told him it was the castor-oil plant, he smiled at the remembrance of the trials that plant had caused him in younger days. One elegant tree, straight as a pine, rose fifty feet in height, with leaves away up at the top only. This was the betel-nut tree.

"The nuts of that tree," said Mr. Ritchie, standing and pointing away up to where the sunlight filtered through the far-off leaves, "are the chewing tobacco of Formosa and all the islands about here. The Chinese do not chew it, but the Malayans do. You will meet some of these natives soon."

On every side grew the rattan, half tree, half vine. It started off as a tree and grew straight up often to twenty feet in height, and then spread itself out over the tops of other trees and plants in vine-like fashion; some of its branches measured almost five hundred feet in length.

The travelers paused to admire one high up in the branches of the trees.

"Many a Chinaman loses his head hunting that plant," remarked Mr. Ritchie. "These islanders export a great deal of rattan, and the head-hunters up there in the mountains watch for the Chinese when they are working in the forest."

Mackay listened eagerly to his friends' tales of the head-hunting savages, living in the mountains. They were always on the lookout for the farmers near their forest lairs. They watched for any unwary man who went too near the woods, pounced upon him, and went off in triumph with his head in a bag.

The young traveler's eyes brightened, "I'll visit them some day!" he cried, looking off toward the mountainside. Mr. Ritchie glanced quickly at the flashing eyes and the quick, alert figure of the young man as he strode along, and some hint came to him of the dauntless young heart which beat beneath that coat of Canadian gray.

Two days more over hill and dale, through rice and tea and tobacco-fields, and then, in the middle of a hot afternoon, Mr. Ritchie began to shiver and shake as though half frozen. Dr. Dickson understood, and at the next stopping-place he ordered a sedan-chair and four coolies to carry it. It was the old dreaded disease that hangs like a black cloud over lovely Formosa, the malarial fever. Mr. Ritchie had been a missionary only four years in the island, but already the scourge had come upon him, and his system was weakened. For, once seized by malaria in Formosa, one seldom makes his escape. They put the sick man into the chair, now in a raging fever, and he was carried by the four coolies.

They were nearing the end of their journey and were now among a people not Chinese. They belonged to the original Malayan race of the island. They had been conquered by the Chinese, who in the early days came over from China under a pirate named Koxinga. As the Chinese name every one but themselves "barbarians," they gave this name to all the natives of the island. They had conquered all but the dreaded head-hunters, who, free in their mountain fastnesses, took a terrible toll of heads from their would-be conquerors, or even from their own half-civilized brethren.

The native Malayans who had been subdued by the Chinese were given different names. Those who lived on the great level rice-plain over which the missionaries were traveling, were called Pe-po-hoan, "Barbarians of the plain." Mackay could see little difference between them and the Chinese, except in the cast of their features, and their long-shaped heads. They wore Chinese dress, even to the cue, worshiped the Chinese gods, and spoke with a peculiar Malayan twang.

The travelers were journeying rather wearily over a low muddy stretch of ground, picking their way along the narrow paths between the rice-fields, when they saw a group of men come hurrying down the path to meet them. They kept calling out, but the words they used were not the familiar "foreign devil" or "ugly barbarian." Instead the people were shouting words of joyful welcome.

Dr. Dickson hailed them with delight, and

soon he and Mr. Ritchie's sedan-chair were surrounded by a clamorous group of friends.

They had journeyed so far south that they had arrived at the borders of the English Presbyterian mission, and the people crowding about them were native Christians. It was all so different from their treatment by the heathen that Mackay's heart was warmed. When the great stone of heathenism was broken, what love and kindness were revealed!

The visitors were led in triumph to the village. There was a chapel here, and they stayed nearly a week, preaching and teaching.

The rest did Mr. Ritchie much good, and at the end of their visit he was once more able to start off on foot. They moved on from village to village and everywhere the Pe-po-hoan Christians received them with the greatest hospitality.

But at last the three friends found the time had come for them to part. The two Englishmen had to go on through their fields to their south Formosan home and the young

Canadian must go back to fight the battle alone in the north of the island. He had endeared himself to the two older men, and when the farewells came they were filled with regret.

They bade him a lingering good-by, with many blessings upon his young head, and many prayers for success in the hard fight upon which he was entering. They walked a short way with him, and stood watching the straight, lithe young figure, so full of courage and hope until it disappeared down the valley. They knew only too well the dangers and trials ahead of him, but they knew also that he was not going into the fight alone. For the Captain was going with his young soldier.

There was a suspicion of moisture in the eyes of the older missionaries as they turned back to prepare for their own journey southward.

"God bless the boy!" said Dr. Dickson fervently. "We'll hear of that young fellow yet, Ritchie. He's on fire."

BEGINNING THE SIEGE

CHAPTER IV

BEGINNING THE SIEGE

THE news was soon noised about Tamsui that one of the three barbarians who had so lately visited the town had returned to make the place his home. This was most unwelcome tidings to the heathen, and the air was filled with mutterings and threatenings, and every one was determined to drive the foreign devil out if at all possible.

So Mackay found himself meeting every kind of opposition. He was too independent to ask assistance from the British consul in the old Dutch fort on the bluff, or of any other European settlers in Tamsui. He was bound to make his own way. But it was not easy to do so in view of the forces which opposed him. He had now been in Formosa about two months and had studied the Chinese language every waking hour, but it was very difficult, and he found his usually ready tongue wofully handicapped.

His first concern was to get a dwelling-place, and he went from house to house inquiring for some place to rent. Everywhere he went he was turned away with rough abuse, and occasionally the dogs were set upon him.

But at last he was successful. Up on the bank of the river, a little way from the edge of the town, he found a place which the owner condescended to rent. It was a miserable little hut, half house, half cellar, built into the side of the hill facing the river. A military officer had intended it for his horse-stable, and yet Mackay paid for this hovel the sum of fifteen dollars a month. It had three rooms, one without a floor. The road ran past the door, and a few feet beyond was the river. By spending money rather liberally he managed to hire the coolie who had accompanied him to south Formosa. With his servant's help Mackay had his new establishment thoroughly cleaned and whitewashed, and then he moved in his furniture. He laughed as he called it furniture, for it consisted of but two packing boxes full of books and clothing. But more came later. The British consul, Mr. Frater, lent him a chair and a bed. There was one old Chinese, who kept a shop near by, and who seemed inclined to be friendly to the queer barbarian with the black beard. He presented him with an old pewter lamp, and the house was furnished complete.

Mackay sat down at his one table, the first night after he was settled. The damp air was hot and heavy, and swarms of tormenting mosquitoes filled the room. Through the open door came the murmur of the river, and from far down in the village the sounds of harsh, clamorous voices. He was alone, many, many miles from home and friends. Around him on every side were bitter enemies.

One might have supposed he would be overcome at the thought of the stupendous task before him, but whoever supposed that did not know George Mackay. He lighted his pewter lamp, opened his diary, and these are the words he wrote:

"Here I am in this house, having been led all the way from the old homestead in Zorra by Jesus, as direct as though my boxes were labeled, 'Tamsui, Formosa, China.' Oh, the glorious privilege to lay the foundation of Christ's Church in unbroken heathenism! God help me to do this with the open Bible! Again I swear allegiance to thee, O King Jesus, my Captain. So help me God!"

And now his first duty was to learn the Chinese language. He could already speak a little, but it would be a long time, he knew, before he could preach. And yet, how was he to learn? he asked himself. He was a scholar without a teacher or school. But there was his servant, and nothing daunted by the difficulties to be overcome, he set to work to make him his teacher also.

George Mackay always went at any task with all his might and main, and he attacked the Chinese language in the same manner. He found it a hard stone to break, however. "Of all earthly things I know of," he remarked once, "it is the most intricate and difficult to master."

His unwilling teacher was just about as hard to manage as his task, for the coolie did not take kindly to giving lessons. He certainly had a rather hard time. Day and night his master deluged him with questions. He made him repeat phrases again and again until his pupil could say them correctly. He asked him the name of everything inside the house and out, until the easy-going Oriental was overcome with dismay. This wild barbarian, with the fiery eyes and the black beard, was a terrible creature who gave one no rest night nor day. Sometimes after Mackay had spent hours with him, imitating sounds and repeating the names of things over and over, his harassed teacher would back out of the room stealthily, keeping an anxious eye on his master, and showing plainly he had grave fears that the foreigner had gone quite mad.

Mackay realized that the pace was too hard for his servant, and that the poor fellow was in a fair way to lose what little wits he had, if not left alone occasionally. So one day he wandered out along the river-bank, in search of some one who would talk with him. He turned into a path that led up the hill behind the town. He was in hopes he might meet a farmer who would be friendly.

When he reached the top of the bluff he found a grassy common stretching back toward the rice-fields. Here and there over these downs strayed the queer-looking water-buffaloes. Some of them were plunged deep in pools of water, and lay there like pigs with only their noses out.

He heard a merry laugh and shout from another part of the common, and there sat a crowd of frolicsome Chinese boys, in large sun hats, and short loose trousers. There were about a dozen of them, and they were supposed to be herding the water-buffaloes to keep them out of the unfenced fields. But, boylike, they were flying kites, and letting their huge-horned charges herd themselves.

Mackay walked over toward them. It was not so long since he had been a boy himself, and these jolly lads appealed to him. But the moment one caught sight of the stranger, he gave a shout of alarm. The rest jumped up, and with yells of terror and cries of "Here's the foreign devil!" "Run, or the foreign devil will get you!" away they went helter-skelter, their big hats waving, their loose clothes flapping wildly. They all disappeared like magic behind a big boulder, and the cause of their terror had to walk away.

But the next day, when his servant once more showed signs of mental exhaustion, he strolled out again upon the downs. The boys were there and saw him coming. Though they did not actually run away this time, they retired to a safe distance, and stood ready to fly at any sign of the barbarian's approach. They watched him wonderingly. They noticed his strange white face, his black beard, his hair cut off quite short, his amazing hat, and his ridiculous clothes. And when at last he walked away, and all danger was over, they burst into shouts of laughter.

The next day, as they scampered about the common, here again came the absurd-looking stranger, walking slowly, as though careful not to frighten them. The boys did not run away this time, and to their utter astonishment he spoke to them. Mackay had practised carefully the words he was to say to them, and the well-spoken Chinese astounded the lads as much as if one of the monkeys that gamboled about the trees of their forests should come down and say, "How do you do, boys?"

"Why, he speaks our words!" they all cried at once.

As they stood staring, Mackay took out his watch and held it up for them to see. It glittered in the sun, and at the sight of it and the kind smiling face above, they lost their fears and crowded around him. They examined the watch in great wonder. They handled his clothes, exclaimed over the buttons on his coat, and inquired what they were for. They felt his hands and his fingers, and finally decided that, in spite of his queer looks, he was after all a man.

From that day the young missionary and the herd-boys were great friends. Every day he joined them in the buffalo pasture, and would spend from four to five hours with them. And as they were very willing to talk, he not only learned their language rapidly, but also learned much about their homes, their schools, their customs, and their religion.

One day, after a lengthy lesson from his servant, the latter decided that the barbarian was unbearable, and bundling up his clothes he marched off, without so much as "by your leave." So Mackay fell back entirely upon his little teachers on the common. With their assistance in the daytime and his Chinese-English dictionary at night, he made wonderful progress.

He was left alone now, to get his own meals and keep the swarms of flies and the damp mold out of his hut by the riverside. He soon learned to eat rice and water-buffalo meat, but he missed the milk and butter and cheese of his old Canadian home. For he discovered that cows were never milked in Formosa. There was variety of food, however, as almost every kind of vegetable that he had ever tasted and many new kinds that he found delicious were for sale in the open-fronted shops in the village. Then the fruits! They were fresh at all seasons—oranges the whole year, bananas fresh from the fields—and such pineapples! He realized that he had never really tasted pineapples before.

Meanwhile, he was becoming acquainted. All the families of the herd-boys learned to like him, and when others came to know him they treated him with respect. He was a teacher, they learned, and in China a teacher is always looked upon with something like reverence. And, besides, he had a beard. This appendage was considered very honorable among Chinese, so the black-bearded barbarian was respected because of this.

But there was one class that treated him with the greatest scorn. These were the

Chinese scholars. They were the literati, and were like princes in the land. They despised every one who was not a graduate of their schools, and most of all they despised this barbarian who dared to set himself up as a teacher. Mackay had now learned Chinese well enough to preach, and his sermons aroused the indignation of these proud graduates.

Sometimes when one was passing the little hut by the river, he would drop in, and glance around just to see what sort of place the barbarian kept. He would pick up the Bible and other books, throw them on the floor, and with words of contempt strut proudly out.

Mackay endured this treatment patiently, but he set himself to study their books, for he felt sure that the day was not far distant when he must meet these conceited literati in argument.

He went about a good deal now. The Tamsui people became accustomed to him, and he was not troubled much. His bright eyes were always wide open and he learned much of the lives of the people he had come to teach. Among the poor he found a poverty of which he had never dreamed. They could live upon what a so-called poor family in Canada would throw away. Nothing was wasted in China. He often saw the meat and fruit tins he threw away when they were emptied, reappearing in the market-place. He learned that these poorer people suffered cruel wrongs at the hands of their magistrates. He visited a yamen, or court-house, and saw the mandarin dispense "justice," but his judgment was said to be always given in favor of the one who paid him the highest bribe. He saw the widow robbed, and the innocent suffering frightful tortures, and sometimes he strode home to his little hut by the river, his blood tingling with righteous indignation. And then he would pray with all his soul:

"O God, give me power to teach these people of thy love through Jesus Christ!"

But of all the horrors of heathenism, and there were many, he found the religion the most dreadful. He had read about it when on board ship, but he found it was infinitely worse when written in men's lives than when set down in print. He never realized what a blessing was the religion of Jesus Christ to a nation until he lived among a people who did not know Him.

He found almost as much difficulty in learning the Chinese religion as the Chinese language. After he had spent days trying to understand it, it would seem to him like some horrible nightmare filled with wicked devils and no less wicked gods and evil spirits and ugly idols. And to make matters worse there was not one religion, but a bewildering mixture of three. First of all there was the ancient Chinese religion, called Confucianism. Confucius, a wise man of China, who lived ages before, had laid down some rules of conduct, and had been worshiped ever since. Very good rules they were as far as they went, and if the Chinese had followed this wise man they would not have drifted so far from the truth. But Confucianism meant ancestor-worship. In every home was a little tablet with the names of the family's ancestors upon it, and every one in the house worshiped the spirits of those departed. With this was another religion called Taoism. This taught belief in wicked demons who lurked about people ready to do them some ill. Then, years and years before, some people from India had brought over their religion, Buddhism, which had become a system of idol-worship. These three religions were so mixed up that the people themselves were not able to distinguish between them. The names of their idols would cover pages, and an account of their religion would fill volumes. The more Mackay learned of it, the more he yearned to tell the people of the one God who was Lord and Father of them all.

As soon as he had learned to write clearly, he bought a large sheet of paper, and printed on it the ten commandments in Chinese characters. Then he hung it on the outside of his door. People who passed read it and made comments of various kinds. Several threw mud at it, and at last a proud graduate, who came striding past, his silk robes rustling grandly, caught the paper and tore it down. Mackay promptly put up another. It shared the fate of the first. Then he put up a third, and the people let it alone. Even these heathen Chinese were beginning to get an impression of the dauntless determination of the man with whom they were to get much better acquainted.

And all this time, while he was studying and working and arguing with the heathen and preaching to them, the young missionary was working just as hard at something else; something into which he was putting as much energy and force as he did into learning the Chinese language. With all his might and main, day and night, he was praying—praying for one special object. He had been praying for this long before he saw Formosa. He was pleading with God to give him, as his first convert, a young man of education. And so he was always on the lookout for such, as he preached and taught, and never once did he cease praying that he might find him.

One forenoon he was sitting at his books,

near the open door, when a visitor stopped before him. It was a fine-looking young man, well dressed and with all the unmistakable signs of the scholar. He had none of the graduate's proud insolence, however, for when Mackay arose, he spoke in the most gentlemanly manner. At the missionary's invitation he entered, and sat down, and the two chatted pleasantly. The visitor seemed interested in the foreigner, and asked him many questions that showed a bright, intelligent mind. When he arose to go, Mackay invited him to come again, and he promised he would. He left his card, a strip of pink paper about three inches by six; the name on it read Giam Cheng Hoa. Mackay was very much interested in him, he was so bright, so affable, and such pleasant company. He waited anxiously to see if he would return.

At the appointed hour the visitor was at the door, and the missionary welcomed him warmly. The second visit was even more pleasant than the first. And Mackay told his guest why he had come to Formosa, and of Jesus Christ who was both God and man and who had come to the earth to save mankind.

The young man's bright eyes were fixed steadily upon the missionary as he talked, and when he went away his face was very thoughtful. Mackay sat thinking about him long after he had left.

He had met many graduates, but none had impressed him as had this youth, with his frank face and his kind, genial manner. There was something too about the young fellow, he felt, that marked him as superior to his companions. And then a sudden divine inspiration flashed into the lonely young missionary's heart. *This was his man!* This was the man for whom he had been praying. The stranger had as yet shown no sign of conversion, but Mackay could not get away from that inspired thought. And that night he could not sleep for joy.

In a day or two the young man returned. With him was a noted graduate, who asked many questions about the new religion. The next day he came again with six graduates, who argued and discussed.

When they were gone Mackay paced up and down the room and faced the serious situation which he realized he was in. He saw plainly that the educated men of the town were banded together to beat him in argument. And with all his energy and desperate determination he set to work to be ready for them.

His first task was to gain a thorough knowledge of the Chinese religions. He had already learned much about them, both from books on shipboard and since he had come to the island. But now he spent long hours of the night, poring over the books of Confucianism, Buddhism, and Taoism, by the light of his smoky little pewter lamp. And before the next visit of his enemies he knew almost more of their jumble of religions than they did themselves.

It was well he was prepared, for his opponents came down upon him in full force. Every day a band of college graduates, always headed by Giam Cheng Hoa, came up from the town to the missionary's little hut by the river, and for hours they would sit arguing and talking. They were always the most noted scholars the place could produce, but in spite of all their cleverness the barbarian teacher silenced them every time. He fairly took the wind out of their sails by showing he knew quite as much about Chinese religions as they did. If they quoted Confucius to contradict the Bible, he would quote Confucius to contradict them. He confounded them by proving that they were not really followers of Confucius, for they did not keep his sayings. And with unanswerable arguments he went on to show that the religion taught by Jesus Christ was the one and only religion to make man good and noble.

Each day the group of visitors grew larger, and at last one morning, as Mackay looked out of his door, he saw quite a crowd approaching. They were led, as usual, by the friendly young scholar. By his side walked, or rather, swaggered a man of whom the missionary had often heard. He was a scholar of high degree and was famed all over Formosa for his great learning. Behind him came about twenty men, and Mackay could see by their dress and appearance that they were all literary graduates. They were coming in great force this time, to crush the barbarian with their combined knowledge. He met them at the door with his usual politeness and hospitality. He was always courteous to these proud literati, but he always treated them as equals, and showed none of the deference they felt he owed them. The crowd seated itself on improvised benches and the argument opened.

This time Mackay led the attack. He carried the war right into the enemy's camp. Instead of letting them put questions to him, he asked them question after question concerning Confucianism, Buddhism, and Taoism. They were questions that sometimes they could not answer, and to their chagrin they had to hear "the barbarian" answer for them. There were other questions, still more humiliating, which, when they answered, only served to show their religion as false and degrading. Their spokesman, the great learned man, became at last so entangled that there was nothing for him but flight. He arose and stalked angrily away, and in a little while they all left. Mackay looked wistfully at young Giam as he went out, wondering what effect these words had upon him.

He was not left long in doubt. Not half an hour after a shadow fell across the open Bible the missionary was studying. He glanced up. There he stood! His bright face was very serious. He looked gravely at the other young man, and his eyes shone as he spoke.

"I brought all those graduates and teachers here," he confessed, "to silence you or be silenced. And now I am convinced that the doctrines you teach are true. I am determined to become a Christian, even though I suffer death for it."

Mackay rose from his seat, his face alight with an overwhelming joy. The man he had prayed for! He took the young fellow's hand—speechless. And together the only missionary of north Formosa and his first convert fell upon their knees before the true God and poured out their hearts in joy and thanksgiving.

SOLDIERS TWO

CHAPTER V

SOLDIERS TWO

AND now a new day dawned for the lonely young missionary. He had not only a convert but a helper and a delightful companion. His new friend was of a bright, joyous nature, the sort that everybody loves. Giam was his surname, but almost every one called him by his given name, Hoa, and those who knew him best called him A Hoa. Mackay used this more familiar boyish name, for Giam was the younger by a few years.

To A Hoa his new friend was always Pastor Mackay, or as the Chinese put it, Mackay Pastor, Kai Bok-su was the real Chinese of it, and Kai Bok-su soon became a name known all over the island of Formosa.

A Hoa needed all his kind new friend's help in the first days after his conversion. For family, relatives, and friends turned upon him with the bitterest hatred for taking up the barbarian's religion. So, driven from his friends, he came to live in the little hut by the river with Mackay. While at home these two read, sang, and studied together all the day long. It would have been hard for an observer to guess who was teacher and who pupil. For at one time A Hoa was receiving Bible instruction and the next time Mackay was being drilled in the Chinese of the educated classes. Each teacher was as eager to instruct as each pupil was eager to learn.

The Bible was, of course, the chief text-book, but they studied other things, astronomy, geology, history, and similar subjects. One day the Canadian took out a map of the world, and the Chinese gazed with amazement at the sight of the many large countries outside China. A Hoa had been private secretary to a mandarin, and had traveled much in China, and once spent six months in Peking. His idea had been that China was everything, that all countries outside it were but insignificant barbarian places. His geography lessons were like revelations.

His progress was simply astonishing, as was also Mackay's. The two seemed possessed with the spirit of hard work. But a superstitious old man who lived near believed they were possessed with a demon. He often listened to the two singing, drilling, and repeating words as they marched up and down, either in the house or in front of it, and he became alarmed. He was a kindly old fellow, and, though a heathen, felt well disposed toward the missionary and A Hoa. So one day, very much afraid, he slipped over to the little house with two small cups of strong tea. He came to the door and proffered them with a polite bow. He hoped they might prove soothing to the disturbed nerves of the patients, he said. He suggested, also, that a visit to the nearest temple might help them.

The two affected ones received his advice politely, but the humor of it struck them both, and when their visitor was gone they laughed so hard the tea nearly choked them.

The missionary was soon able to speak so fluently that he preached almost every day, either in the little house by the river, or on the street in some open square. There were other things he did, too. On every side he saw great suffering from disease. The chief malady was the terrible malaria, and the native doctors with their ridiculous remedies only made the poor sufferers worse. Mackay had studied medicine for a short time while in college, and now found his knowledge very useful. He gave some simple remedies to several victims of malaria which proved effective. The news of the cures spread far and wide. The barbarian was kind, he had a good heart, the people declared. Many more came to him for medicine, and day by day the circle of his friends grew. And wherever he went, curing disease, teaching, or preaching, A Hoa went with him, and shared with him the taunts of their heathen enemies.

But the gospel was gradually making its way. Not long after A Hoa's conversion a second man confessed Christ. He had previously disturbed the meetings by throwing stones into the doorway whenever he passed. But his sister was cured of malaria by the missionary's medicine, and soon both sister and mother became Christians, and finally the stone-thrower himself. And so, gradually, the lines of the enemy were falling back, and at every sign of retreat the little army of two advanced. A little army? No! For was there not the whole host of heaven moving with them? And Mackay was learning that his boyish dreams of glory were truly to be fulfilled. He had wanted always to be a soldier like his grandfather, and fight a great Waterloo, and here he was right in the midst of the battle with the victory and the glory sure.

The two missionaries often went on short trips here and there into the country around Tamsui, and Mackay determined that when the intense summer heat had lessened they would make a long tour to some of the large cities. The heat of August was almost overpowering to the Canadian. Flies and mosquitoes and insect pests of all kinds made his life miserable, too, and prevented his studying as hard as he wished.

One oppressive day he and A Hoa returned from a preaching tour in the country to find their home in a state of siege. Right across the threshold lay a monster serpent, eight feet in length. A Hoa shouted a warning, and seized a long pole, and the two managed to kill it. But their troubles were not yet over. The next morning, Mackay stepped outside the door and sprang back just in time to escape another, the mate of the one killed. This one was even larger than the first, and was very fierce. But they finished it with sticks and stones.

When September came the days grew clearer, and the many pests of summer were not so numerous. The mosquitoes and flies that had been such torments disappeared, and there was some relief from the damp oppressive heat. But he had only begun to enjoy the refreshing breaths of cool air, and had remarked to A Hoa that the days reminded him of Canadian summers, when the weather gave him to understand that every

"We shall Go to Kelung First"

Formosan season has its drawbacks. September brought tropical storms and typhoons that were terrible, and he saw from his little house on the hillside big trees torn up by the root, buildings swept away like chaff, and out in the harbor great ships lifted from their anchorage and whirled away to destruction. And then he was sometimes thankful that his little hut was built into the hillside, solid and secure.

But the fierce storms cleared away the heavy dampness that had made the heat of the summer so unbearable, and October and November brought delightful days. The weather was still warm of course, but the nights were cool and pleasant.

So early one October morning, Mackay and A Hoa started off on a tour to the cities.

"We shall go to Kelung first," said the missionary. Kelung was a seaport city on the northern coast, straight east across the island from Tamsui. A coolie to carry food and clothing was hired, and early in the morning, while the stars were still shining, they passed through the sleeping town and out on the little paths between the rice-fields.

Though it was yet scarcely daylight, the farmers were already in their fields. It was harvest-time—the second harvest of the year—and the little rice-fields were no longer like mirrors, but were filled with high rustling grain ready for the sickle. The water had been drained off and the reaper and thrasher were going through the fields before dawn. There was no machinery like that used at home. The reaper was a short sickle, the thrashing-machine a kind of portable tub, and Mackay looked at them with some amusement, and described to A Hoa how they took off the great wheat crops in western Canada.

The two were in high spirits, ready for any sort of adventure and they met some. Toward evening they reached a place called Sek-khau, and went to the little brick inn to get a sleeping-place. The landlord came to the door and was about to bid A Hoa enter, when the light fell upon Mackay's face. With a shout, "Black-bearded barbarian!" he slammed the door in their faces. They turned away, but already a crowd had begun to gather. "The black-bearded barbarian is here! The foreign devil from Tamsui has come!" was the cry. The mob followed the two down the streets, shouting curses. Some one threw a broken piece of brick, another a stone. Mackay turned and faced them, and for a few moments they seemed cowed. But the crowd was increasing, and he deemed it wise to move on. So the two marched out of the town followed by stones and curses. And, as they went, Mackay reminded A Hoa of what they had been reading the night before.

"Yes," said A Hoa brightly. "The Lord Jesus was driven out of his own town in Galilee."

"Yes, and Paul—you remember how he was stoned. Our Master counts us worthy to suffer for him."

But where to go was the question. Before they could decide, night came down upon them, and it came in that sudden tropical way to which Mackay, all his life accustomed to the long mellow twilights of his northern home, could never grow accustomed. They each took a torch out of the carrier's bag, lighted it, and marched bravely on. The path led along the Kelung river, through tall grass. They were not sure where it led to, but thought it wise to follow the river; they would surely come to Kelung some time. Mackay was ahead, A Hoa right at his heels, and behind them the basket-bearer. At a sudden turn in the path A Hoa gave a shout of warning, and the next instant, a band of robbers leaped from the long reeds and grass, and brandished their spears in the travelers' faces. The torch-light shone on their fierce evil eyes and their long knives, making a horrible picture. The young Canadian Scot did not flinch for a second. He looked the wild leader straight in the face.

"We have no money, so you cannot rob us," he said steadily, "and you must let us pass at once. I am a teacher and——"

"A *teacher!"* he was interrupted by a dismayed exclamation from several of the wild band. "A teacher!" As if with one accord they turned and fled into the darkness. For even a highwayman in China respects a man of learning. The travelers went on again, with something of relief and something of the exultation that youth feels in having faced danger. But a second trouble was upon them. One of those terrible storms that still raged occasionally had been brewing all evening, and now it opened its artillery. Great howling gusts came down from the mountain, carrying sheets of driving rain. Their torches went out like matches, and they were left to stagger along in the black darkness. What were they to do? They could not go back. They could not stay there. They scarcely dared go on. For they did not know the way, and any moment a fresh blast of wind or a misstep might hurl them into the river. But they decided that they must go on, and on they went, stumbling, slipping, sprawling, and falling outright. Now there would be an exclamation from Mackay as he sank to the knees in the mud of a rice-field, now a groan from A Hoa as he fell over a boulder and bruised and scratched himself, and oftenest a yell from the poor coolie, as he slipped, baskets and all, into some rocky crevice, and was sure he was tumbling into the river; but they staggered on, Mackay secure in his faith in God. His Father knew and his Father would keep him safely. And behind him came brave young A Hoa, buoyed up by his new growing faith, and learning the lesson that sometimes the Captain asks his soldier to march into hard encounters, but that the soldier must never flinch.

The "everlasting arms" were around them, for by midnight they reached Kelung. They were drenched, breathless, and worn out, and they spent the night in a damp hovel, glad of any shelter from the wind and rain.

But the next morning, young soldier A Hoa had a fiercer battle to fight than any with robbers or storms. As soon as the city was astir, Mackay and he went out to find a good place to preach. They passed down the main thoroughfare, and everywhere they attracted attention. Cries of "Ugly barbarian!" and oftenest "Black-bearded barbarian" were heard on all sides. A Hoa was known in Kelung and contempt and ridicule was heaped upon him by his old college acquaintances. He was consorting with the barbarian! He was a friend of this foreigner! They poured more insults upon him than they did upon the barbarian himself. Some took the stranger as a joke, and laughed and made funny remarks upon his appearance. Here and there an old woman, peeping through the doorway, would utter a loud cackling laugh, and pointing a wizened finger at the missionary would cry: "Eh, eh, look at him! Tee hee! He's got a wash-basin on for a hat!" A Hoa was distressed at these remarks, but Mackay was highly amused.

"We're drawing a crowd, anyway," he remarked cheerfully, "and that's what we want."

Soon they came to an open square in front of a heathen temple. The building had several large stone steps leading up to the door. Mackay mounted them and stood facing the buzzing crowd, with A Hoa at his side. They started a hymn:

> All people that on earth do dwell
> Sing to the Lord with cheerful voice.

The open square in front of them began to fill rapidly. The people jostled each other in their endeavors to get a view of the barbarian. Every one was curious, but every one was angry and indignant, so sometimes the sound of the singing was lost in the shouts of derision.

When the hymn was finished, Mackay had a sudden inspiration. "They will surely listen to one of their own people," he said to himself, and turned to A Hoa.

"Speak to them," he said. "Tell them about the true God."

That was a hard moment for the young convert. He had been a Christian only a few months and had never yet spoken in public for Christ. He looked desperately over the sea of mocking faces beneath him. He opened his mouth, as though to speak, and hesitated. Just then came a rough and bitter taunt from one of his old companions. It was too much. A Hoa turned away and hung his head.

The young missionary said nothing. But he did the very wisest thing he could have done. He had some time before taught A Hoa a grand old Scottish paraphrase, and they had often sung it together:

I'm not ashamed to own my Lord
  Or to defend his cause,
Maintain the glory of his cross
  And honor all his laws.

Mackay's voice, loud and clear, burst into this fine old hymn. A Hoa raised his head. He joined in the hymn and sang it to the end. It put mettle into him. It was the battle-song that brought back the young recruit's courage. Almost before the last note sounded he began to speak. His voice rang out bold and unafraid over the crowd of angry heathen.

"I am a Christian!" he said distinctly. "I worship the true God. I cannot worship idols," with a gesture toward the temple door, "that rats can destroy. I am not afraid. I love Jesus. He is my Savior and Friend."

No, A Hoa was not "ashamed" any more. His testing time had come, and he had not failed after all. And his brave, true words sent a thrill of joy through the more seasoned soldier at his side.

That was not the only difficult situation he met on that journey. The two soldiers of the cross had many trials, but the thrill of that victory before the Kelung temple never left them.

When they returned to Tamsui they held daily services in their house, and A Hoa often spoke to the people who gathered there.

One Sunday they noticed an old woman present, who had come down the river in a boat. Women as a rule did not come out to the meetings, but this old lady continued to come every Sunday. She showed great interest in the missionary's words, and, at the close of one meeting, he spoke to her. She told him she was a poor widow, that her name was Thah-so, and that she had come down the river from Go-ko-khi to hear him preach. Then she added, "I have passed through many trials in this world, and my idols never gave me any comfort." Then her eyes shone, "But I like your teaching very much," she went on. "I believe the God you tell about will give me peace. I will come again, and bring others."

Next Sunday she was there with several other women. And after that she came every Sunday, bringing more each time, until at last a whole boat-load would come down to the service.

These people were so interested that they asked the missionary if he would not visit them. So one day he and A Hoa boarded one of the queer-looking flat-bottomed river boats and were pulled up the rapids to Go-ko-khi. Every village in Formosa had its headman, who is virtually the ruler of the place. When the boat landed, many of the villagers were at the shore to meet their visitors and took them at once to their mayor's house, the best building in the village. Tan

Paugh, a fine, big, powerfully-built man, received them cordially. He frankly declared that he was tired and sick of idols and wanted to hear more of this new religion. An empty granary was obtained for both church and home, and the missionary and his assistant took up their quarters there, and for several months they remained, preaching and teaching the Bible either in Go-ho-khi, or in the lovely surrounding valleys.

THE GREAT KAI BOK-SU

CHAPTER VI

THE GREAT KAI BOK-SU

THE missionary was now becoming a familiar figure both in Tamsui and in the surrounding country. By many he was loved, by all he was respected, but by a large number he was bitterly hated. The scholars continued his worst enemies. They could never forgive him for beating them so completely in argument, in the days when A Hoa was striving for the light, and their hatred increased as they saw other scholars becoming Christians under his teaching. There was something about him, however, that compelled their respect and even their admiration. Wherever they met him—on the street, by their temples, or on the country roads—he bore himself in such a way as to make them confess that he was their superior both in ability and knowledge.

These Chinese literati had a custom which Mackay found very interesting. One proud scholar marching down the street and scarcely noticing the obsequious bows of his inferiors, would meet another equally proud scholar. Each would salute the other in an exceedingly grand manner, and then one would spin off a quotation from the writings of Confucius or some other Chinese sage and say, "Now tell me where that is found." And scholar number two had to ransack his brains to remember where the saying was found, or else confess himself beaten. Mackay thought it might be a good habit for the graduates of his own alma mater across the wide sea to adopt. He wondered what some of his old college chums would think, if, when he got back to Canada, he should buttonhole one on the street some day, recite a quotation from Shakespeare or Macaulay, and demand from his friend where it could be found. He had a suspicion that the old friend would be afraid that the Oriental sun had touched George Mackay's brain.

Nevertheless he thought the custom one he

could turn to good account, and before long he was trying it himself. He had such a wonderful memory that he never forgot anything he had once read. So the scholars of north Formosa soon discovered, again to their humiliation, that this Kai Bok-su of Tamsui could beat them at their own game. They did not care how much he might profess to know of writers and lands beyond China. Such were only barbarians anyway. But when, right before a crowd, he would display a surer knowledge of the Chinese classics than they themselves, they began not only to respect but to fear him. It was no use trying to humiliate him with a quotation. With his bright eyes flashing, he would tell, without a moment's hesitation, where it was found and come back at the questioner swiftly with another, most probably one long forgotten, and reel it off as though he had studied Chinese all his life.

He was a wonderful man certainly, they all agreed, and one whom it was not safe to oppose. The common people liked him better every day. He was so tactful, so kind, and always so careful not to arouse the prejudice of the heathen. He was extremely wise in dealing with their superstitions. No matter how absurd or childish they might be, he never ridiculed them, but only strove to show the people how much happier they might be if they believed in God as their Father and in Jesus Christ as their Savior. He never made light of anything sacred to the Chinese mind, but always tried to take whatever germ of good he could find in their religion, and lead on from it to the greater good found in Christianity. He discovered that the ancestral worship made the younger people kind and respectful to older folk, and he saw that Chinese children reverenced their parents and elders in a way that he felt many of his young friends across the sea would do well to copy.

One day when he and A Hoa were out on a preaching tour, the wise Kai Bok-su made use of this respect for parents in quieting a mob. He and his comrade were standing side by side on the steps of a heathen temple as they had done at Kelung. The angry crowd was scowling and muttering, ready to throw stones as soon as the preacher uttered a word. Mackay knew this, and when they had sung a hymn and the people waited, ready for a riot, his voice rang out clear and steady, repeating the fifth commandment, "Honor thy father and thy mother: that thy days may be long upon the land which the Lord thy God giveth thee." A silence fell over the muttering crowd, and an old heathen whose cue was white and whose aged hands trembled on the top of his staff, nodded his head and said, "That is heavenly doctrine." The people were surprised and disarmed. If the black-bearded barbarian taught such truths as this, he surely was not so very wicked after all. And so they listened attentively as he went on to show that they had all one great Father, even God.

He sometimes found it rather a task to treat with respect that which the Chinese held sacred. Especially was this so when he discovered to his amusement and to some carefully concealed disgust, that in the Chinese family the pig was looked upon with affection, and as a young naval officer, who visited Mackay remarked, "was treated like a gentleman."

Every Chinese house of any size was made up of three buildings joined together so as to make three sides of an enclosure. This space was called a court, and a door led from it to another next the street. In this outer yard pigs and fowl were always to be found. Whenever the missionary dropped in at a home, mother pig and all the little pigs often followed him inside the house, quite like members of the family. Every one was always glad to see Kai Bok-su, pigs and all, and as soon as he appeared the order was given—"Infuse tea." And when the little handleless cups of clear brown liquid were passed around and they all drank and chatted, Mrs. Pig and her children strolled about as welcome as the guest.

The Chinese would allow no one to hurt their pigs, either. One day as Mackay sat in his rooms facing the river, battling with some new Chinese characters, he heard a great hubbub coming up the street. The threatening mobs that used to surround his house had long ago ceased to trouble him. He arose in some surprise and went to the door to see what was the matter. A very unusual sight for Tamsui met his gaze. Coming up the street at a wild run were some half-dozen English sailors, their loose blue blouses and trousers flapping madly. They were evidently from a ship which Mackay had seen lying in the harbor that morning.

"Give us a gun!" roared the foremost as soon as he saw the missionary.

Mackay did not possess a gun, and would not have given the enraged bluejacket one had he owned a dozen. But the Chinese mob, roaring with fury, were coming up the street after the men and he swiftly pointed out a narrow alley that led down to the river. "Run down there!" he shouted to the sailors. "You can get to your boats before they find you."

They were gone in an instant, and the next moment the crowd of pursuers were storming about the door demanding whither the enemy had disappeared.

"What is all this disturbance about?" demanded Kai Bok-su calmly, glad of an opportunity to gain time for the fleeing sailors.

The aggrieved Chinese gathered about him, each telling the story as loud as his voice would permit. Those barbarians of the sea had come swaggering along the streets waving their big sticks. And they had dared—yes actually *dared*—to hit the pet pigs belonging to every house as they passed. The poor pigs who lay sunning themselves at the door!

This was indeed a serious offense. Mackay could picture the rollicking sailor-lads gaily whacking the lazy porkers with their canes as they passed, happily unconscious of the trouble they were raising. But there was no amusement in Kai Bok-su's grave face. He spoke kindly, and soothingly, and promised that if the offenders misbehaved again he would complain to the authorities. That made it all right. Heathen though they were, they knew Kai Bok-su's promise would not be broken, and away they went quite satisfied.

One day he learned, quite by accident, a new and very useful way of helping his people. He and A Hoa and several other young men who had become Christians, went on a missionary tour to Tek-chham, a large city which he had visited once before.

On the day they left the place, Kai Bok-su's preaching had drawn such crowds that the authorities of the city became afraid of him. And when the little party left, a dozen soldiers were sent to follow the dangerous barbarian and his students and see that they did not bewitch the people on the road.

The soldiers tramped along after the missionary party, and with his usual ability to make use of any situation, Mackay stepped back and chatted with his spies. He found one poor fellow in agony with the toothache. This malady was very common in north Formosa, partly owing to the habit of chewing the betel-nut. He examined the aching tooth and found it badly decayed. "There is a worm in it," the soldier said, for the Formosan doctors had taught the people this was the cause of toothache.

Mackay had no forceps, but he knew how to pull a tooth, and he was not the sort to be daunted by the lack of tools. He got a piece of hard wood, whittled it into shape and with it pried out the tooth. The relief from pain was so great that the soldier almost wept for joy and overwhelmed the tooth-puller with gratitude. And for the remainder of the journey the guards sent to spy on the missionary's doings were his warmest friends.

After this, dentistry became a part of this many-sided missionary's work. He went to a native blacksmith and had a pair of forceps hammered out of iron. It was a rather clumsy instrument, but it proved of great value, and later he sent for a complete set of the best instruments made in New York.

So with forceps in one hand and the Bible in the other, Mackay found himself doubly equipped. Every second person seemed to be suffering from toothache, and when the pain was relieved by the missionary, the

"Next, Any One who Wanted a Tooth Pulled was Invited to Come Forward"

patient was in a state of mind to receive his teaching kindly. The cruel methods by which the native doctors extracted teeth often caused more suffering than the toothache, and sometimes even resulted in death through blood-poisoning.

A Hoa and some of the other young converts learned from their teacher how to pull a tooth, and they, too, became experts in the art.

Whenever they visited a town or city after this, they had a program which they always followed. First they would place themselves in front of an idol temple or in an open square. Here they would sing a hymn which always attracted a crowd. Next, any one who wanted a tooth pulled was invited to come forward. Many accepted the invitation gladly and sometimes a long line of twenty or thirty would be waiting, each his turn. The Chinese had considerable nerve, the Canadian discovered, and stood the pain bravely. They literally "stood" it, too, for there was no dentist's chair and every man stood up for his operation, very much pleased and very grateful when it was over. Then there were quinine and other simple remedies for malaria handed round, for in a Formosan crowd there were often many shaking in the grip of this terrible disease. And now, having opened the people's hearts by his kindness, Kai Bok-su brought forth his cure for souls. He would mount the steps of the temple or stand on a box or stone, and tell the wonderful old story of the man Jesus who was also God, and who said to all sick and weary and troubled ones, "Come unto me, . . . and I will give you rest." And often, when he had finished, the disease of sin in many a heart was cured by the remedy of the gospel.

And so the autumn passed away happily and busily, and Mackay entered his first Formosan winter. And such a winter! The young man who had felt the clear, bright cold of a Canadian January needed all his fine courage to bear up under its dreariness. It started about Christmas time. Just when his own people far away in Canada were gathering about the blazing fire or jingling over the crisp snow in sleighs and cutters, the great winter rains commenced. Christmas day—his first Christmas in a land that did not know its beautiful meaning—was one long dreary downpour. It rained steadily all Christmas week. It poured on New-year's day and for a week after. It came down in torrents all January. February set in and still it rained and rained, with only a short interval each afternoon. Day and night, week in, week out, it poured, until Mackay forgot what sunlight looked like. His house grew damp, his clothes moldy. A stream broke out up in the hill behind and one morning he awoke to find a cascade tumbling into his kitchen, and rushing across the floor out into the river beyond. And still it poured and the wind blew and everything was damp and cold and dreary.

He caught an occasional glimpse of snow, only a very far-off view, for it lay away up on the top of a mountain, but it made his heart long for just one breath of good dry Canadian air, just one whiff of the keen, cutting frost.

But Kai Bok-su was not the sort to spend these dismal days repining. Indeed he had no time, even had he been so inclined. His work filled up every minute of every rainy day and hours of the drenched night. If there was no sunshine outside there was plenty in his brave heart, and A Hoa's whole nature radiated brightness.

And there were many reasons for being happy after all. On the second Sabbath of February, 1873, just one year after his arrival in Tamsui, the missionary announced, at the close of one of his Sabbath services, that he would receive a number into the Christian church. There was instantly a commotion among the heathen who were in the house, and yells and jeers from those crowding about the door outside.

"We'll stop him," they shouted. "Let us beat the converts," was another cry.

But Mackay went quietly on with the beautiful ceremony in spite of the disturbance. Five young men, with A Hoa at their head, came and were baptized into the name of the Father, the Son, and the Holy Spirit.

When the next Sabbath came these five with their missionary sat down for the first time to partake of the Lord's Supper. It was a very impressive ceremony. One young fellow broke down, declaring he was not worthy. Mackay took him alone into his little room and they prayed together, and the young man came out to the Lord's Supper comforted, knowing that all might be worthy in Jesus Christ.

Spring came at last, bright and clear, and Mackay announced to A Hoa that they must go up the river and visit their friends at Go-ko-khi. The two did not go alone this time. Three other young men who wanted to be missionaries were now spending their days with their teacher, learning with A Hoa how to preach the gospel. So it was quite a little band of disciples that walked along the river bank up to Go-ko-khi. Mackay preached at all the villages along the route, and visited the homes of Christians.

One day, as they passed a yamen or Chinese court-house where a mandarin was trying some cases, they stepped in to see what was going on. At one end of the room sat the mandarin who was judge. He was dressed in magnificent silks and looked down very haughtily upon the lesser people and the retinue of servants who were gathered about him. On either side of the room stood a row of constables and near them the executioners. The rest of the room was filled with friends of the people on trial and by the rabble from the street. The missionaries mixed with the former and stood watching proceedings. There were no lawyers, no jury. The mandarin's decision was law.

The first case was one of theft. Whether the man had really committed the crime or not was a question freely discussed among the onlookers around Mackay. But there seemed no doubt as to his punishment being swift and heavy. "He has not paid the mandarin," a friend explained to the missionary. "He will be punished."

"The mandarin eats cash," remarked another with a shrug. It was a saying to which Mackay had become accustomed. For it was one of the shameless proverbs of poor, oppressed Formosa.

The case was soon finished. Nothing was definitely proven against the man. But the mandarin pronounced the sentence of death. The victim was hurried out, shrieking his innocence, and praying for mercy. Case followed case, each one becoming more revolting than the last to the eyes of the young man accustomed to British justice. Imprisonment and torture were meted out to prisoners, and even witnesses were laid hold of and beaten on the face by the executioners if their tale did not suit the mandarin. Men who were plainly guilty but who had given their judge a liberal bribe were let off, while innocent men were made to pay heavy fines or were thrown into prison.

The young missionary went out and on his way sickened by the sights he had witnessed. And as he went, he raised his eyes to heaven and prayed fervently that he might be a faithful preacher of the gospel, and that one day Formosa would be a Christian land and injustice and oppression be done away.

The next scene was a happier one. There was an earnest little band of Christians in Go-ko-khi, and two of the young people were about to be married. It was the first Christian marriage in the place and Kai Bok-su was called upon to officiate. There was a great deal of opposition raised among the heathen, but after seeing the ceremony, they all voted a Christian wedding everything that was beautiful and good.

BESIEGING HEAD-HUNTERS

CHAPTER VII

BESIEGING HEAD-HUNTERS

WHEN they returned from their trip, Mackay and A Hoa with the assistance of some of their Christian friends set about looking for a new house in a more wholesome district. It was much easier for the missionary to rent a place now, and he managed to secure a comfortable home upon the bluff above the town. It was a dryer situation and much more healthful. Here one room was used as a study and every morning when not away on a tour a party of young men gathered in it for lessons. Sometimes, what with traveling, preaching, training his students, visiting the sick, and pulling teeth, Mackay had scarcely time to eat, and very little to sleep. But always as he came and went on his travels, his eyes would wander to the mountains where the savages lived, and with all his heart he would wish that he might visit them also.

His Chinese friends held up their hands in dismay when he broached the subject. To the mountains where the Chhi-hoan lived! Did Kai Bok-su not know that every man of them was a practised head-hunter, and that behind every rock and tree and in the darkness of the forests they lay in wait for any one who went beyond the settled districts? Yes, Kai Bok-su knew all that, but he could not quite explain that it was just that which made the thought of a visit to them seem so alluring, just that which made him so anxious to tell them of Jesus Christ, who wished all men to live as brothers. A Hoa and a few others who had caught the spirit of the true soldier of the cross understood. For they had learned that one who follows Jesus must be ready to dare anything, death included, to carry the news of his salvation to the dark corners of the world.

But the days were so filled with preaching, teaching, and touring, that for some time Mackay had no opportunity for a trip into the head-hunters' territory. And then one day, quite unexpectedly, his chance came.

There sailed into Tamsui harbor, one hot afternoon, a British man-of-war, named *The Dwarf*. Captain Bax from this vessel visited Tamsui, and expressed a desire to see something of the life of the savages in the mountains. This was Mackay's opportunity, and in spite of protests from his friends he offered to accompany the captain. So together they started off, the sailor-soldier of England and the soldier of the cross, each with the same place in view but each with a very different object.

It took three days' journey from Tamsui across rice-fields and up hillsides to reach even the foot of the mountains. Here there lived a village of natives, closely related to the savages. But they were not given to head-hunting and were quite friendly with the people about them. Mackay had met some of these people on a former trip inland, and now he and Captain Bax hired their chief and a party of his men to guide them up into savage territory.

The travelers slept that night in the village, and before dawn were up and ready to start on their dangerous undertaking. Before them in the gray dawn rose hill upon hill, each loftier than the last, till they melted into the mountains, the territory of the dreaded head-hunters. They started off on a steady tramp, up hills, down valleys, and across streams, until at last they came to the foot of the first mountain.

Before them rose its sheer side, towering thirty-five hundred feet above their heads. It was literally covered with rank growth of all kinds, through which it was impossible to move. So a plan of march had to be decided upon. In front went a line of men with long sharp knives. With these they cut away the creepers and tangled scrub or undergrowth. Next came the coolies with the baggage, and last the two travelers. It was slow work, and sometimes the climb was so steep they held their breath, as they crept over a sheer ledge and saw the depth below to which they might easily be hurled. The chief of the guides himself collapsed in one terrible climb, and his men tied rattan ropes about him and hauled him up over the steepest places.

During this wearisome ascent the most untiring one was the missionary; and the sailor often looked at him in amazement. His lithe, wiry frame never seemed to grow weary. He was often in the advance line, cutting his way through the tangle, and here on that first afternoon he met with an unpleasant adventure.

The natives had warned the two strangers to be on the lookout for poisonous snakes, and Mackay's year in Formosa had taught him to be wary. But he had forgotten all danger in the toilsome climb. He was soon reminded of it. They were passing up a slope covered with long dense grass when a rustling at his side made the young missionary pause. The next moment a huge cobra sprang out from a clump of grass and struck at him. Mackay sprang aside just in time to escape its deadly fangs. The guides rushed up with their spears only to see its horrible scaly length disappear in the long grass.

That was not the only escape of the young adventurer, for there were wild animals as well as poisonous snakes along the line of march, and the man in the front was always in danger. But at the front Mackay must be in spite of all warning. Nobody moved fast enough for him.

At last they reached the summit of the range. They were now on the dividing line between Chinese ground and savage territory, and the men who dared go a step farther went at terrible risk. The head-hunters would very likely see that they did not return.

But Mackay was all for pushing forward, and Captain Bax was no less eager. So they spent a night in the forest and the next day marched on up another and higher range. As they journeyed, the travelers could not but burst into exclamations of delight at the loveliness about them. Behind those great trees and in those tangles of vines might lurk the head-hunters, but for all that the beauty of the place made them forget the dangers. The great banyan trees whose branches came down and took root in the earth, making a wonderful round leafy tent, grew on every side. Camphor trees towered far above them and then spread out great branches sixty or seventy feet from the ground. Then there was the rattan creeping out over the tops of the other trees and making a thick canopy through which the hot tropical sun-rays could not penetrate.

And the flowers! Sometimes Mackay and Bax would stand amazed at their beauty. They came one afternoon to an open glade in the cool green dimness of the forest. On all sides the stately tree-ferns rose up thirty or forty feet above them, and underneath grew a tangle of lovely green undergrowth.

And upon this green carpet it seemed to their dazzled eyes that thousands of butterflies of the loveliest form and color had just alighted. And not only butterflies, but birds and huge insects and all sorts of winged creatures, pink and gold and green and scarlet and blue, and all variegated hues. But the lovely things sat motionless, sending out such a delightful perfume that there could be no doubt that they were flowers,—the wonderful orchids of Formosa! Mackay was a keen scientist, always highly interested in botany, and he was charmed with this sight. There were many such in the forest, and often he would stop spellbound before a blaze of flowers hanging from tree or vine or shrub. Then he would look up at the tangled growths of the bamboo, the palm, and the elegant tree-fern, standing there all silent and beautiful, and he would be struck by the harmony between God's work and Word. "I can't keep from studying the flora of Formosa," he said to Captain Bax. "What missionary would not be a better man, the bearer of a richer gospel, what convert would not be a more enduring Christian from becoming acquainted with such wonderful works of the Creator?"

At last they stood on the summit of the second range and saw before them still more mountains, clothed from summit to base

Copyright 1895, by Fleming H. Revell Company "From Far Formosa"

"THE HEAD HUNTERS WERE ARMED TO THE TEETH"

with trees. They were now right in savage territory and their guide clambered out upon a spur of rock and announced that there was a party of head-hunters in the valley below. He gave a long halloo. From away down in the valley came an answering call, ringing through the forest. Then far down through the thicket Mackay's sharp eyes descried the party coming up to meet them. Just then their own guide gave the signal to move on, and the missionary and Captain Bax walked down the hill—the first white men who had ever come out to meet those savages.

Half-way down the slope the two parties came face to face. The head-hunters were a wild, uncouth-looking company, armed to the teeth. They all carried guns, spears, and knives and some had also bows and arrows slung over their backs. Their faces were hideously tattooed in a regular pattern, while they wore no more clothes than were necessary. A sort of sack of coarse linen with holes in the sides for their arms, served as the chief garment, and generally the only one. Every one wore a broad belt of woven rattan in which was stuck his crooked pointed knife. Some of the younger men had their coats ornamented with bright red and blue threads woven into the texture. They had brass rings on their arms and legs too, and even sported big earrings. These were ugly looking things made of bamboo sticks. The head-hunters were all barefooted, but most of them wore caps—queer-looking things, made of rattan. From many of them hung bits of skin of the boar or other wild animals they had killed. They stood staring suspiciously at the two strangers. Never before had they seen a white man, and the appearance of the naval officer and the missionary, so different from themselves, and yet so different from their hated enemies, the Chinese, filled them with amazement and a good deal of suspicion. After a little talk with the guides, however, the visitors were allowed to pass on. As soon as they began to move, the savages fell into line behind them and followed closely. The two white men, walking calmly onward, could not help thinking how easy it would be for one of those fierce-looking tattooed braves to win applause by springing upon both of them and carrying their heads in triumph to the next village.

As they came down farther into the valley, they passed the place where the savages had their camp. Here naked children and tattooed women crept out of the dense woods to stare at the queer-looking Chinamen who had white faces and wore no cue.

The march through this valley, even without the head-hunters at their heels, would not have been easy. The visitors clambered over huge trunks blown across the path, and tore their clothes and hands scrambling through the thorny bushes. The sun was still shining on the mountain-peaks far above them, but away down here in the valley it was rapidly growing dark and very cold. They had almost decided to stop and wait for morning when a light ahead encouraged them to go on. They soon came upon a big camp-fire and round it were squatted several hundred savages. The firelight gleaming upon the dark, fierce faces of the head-hunters and on their spears and knives, made a startling picture.

They were round the visitors immediately, staring at the two white men in amazement. The party of savages who had escorted them seemed to be making some explanation of their appearance, for they all subsided at last and once more sat round their fire.

The newcomers started a fire of their own, and their servants cooked their food. The white men were in momentary danger of their lives. But they sat on the ground before the fire and quietly ate their supper while hundreds of savage eyes were fixed upon them in suspicious, watchful silence.

The meal over the servants prepared a place for the travelers to sleep, and while they were so doing, the young missionary was not idle. He longed to speak to these poor, darkened heathen, but they could not understand Chinese. However, he found several poor fellows lying prostrate on the ground, overcome with malaria, and he got his guide to ask if he might not give the sick ones medicine. Being allowed to do so, he gave each one a dose of quinine. The poor creatures tried to look their gratitude when the terrible chills left them, and soon they were able to sink into sleep.

Before he retired to his own bed of boughs, the young missionary sang that grand old anthem which these lonely woods and their savage inhabitants had never yet heard:

All people that on earth do dwell,
Sing to the Lord with cheerful voice.

But these poor people could not "sing to the Lord," for they had never yet so much as heard his name.

All night the missionary lay on the ground, finding the chill mountain air too cold for sleep, and whenever he looked out from his shelter of boughs he saw hundreds of savage eyes, gleaming in the firelight, still wide open and fixed upon him.

Day broke late in the valley, but the travelers were astir in the morning twilight. The mountain-tops were touched with rosy light even while it was dark down in these forest depths.

The chilled white men were glad to get up and exercise their stiffened limbs. There were several of their party who could speak both Chinese and the dialect of these mountaineers, and through them Mackay persuaded the chief of the tribe to take them to visit his village.

He seemed reluctant at first and there was much discussion with his braves. Evidently they were more anxious to go on a head-hunt than to act the part of hosts. However, after a great deal of chatter, they consented, and the chief and his son with thirty men separated themselves from the rest of the band and led the way out of the valley up the mountainside. The travelers had to stop often, for, besides the natural difficulties of the way, the chief proved a new obstacle. Every mile or so he would apparently repent of his hospitality. He would stop, gather his tattooed braves about him and confer with them, while his would-be visitors sat on the ground or a fallen tree-trunk to await his pleasure. Finally he would start off again, the travelers following, but no sooner were they under way than again their uncertain guide would stop. Once he and his men stood motionless, listening. Away up in the boughs of a camphor tree a little tailor-bird was twittering. The savages listened as though to the voice of an oracle.

"What are they doing?" Mackay asked of one of his men, when the head-hunters stopped a second time and stared earnestly at the boughs above.

"Bird-listening," explained the guide. A few more questions drew from him the fact that the savages believed the little birds would tell them whether or not they should bring these strangers home. They always consulted the birds when starting out on a head-hunt, he further explained. If the birds gave a certain kind of chirp and flew in a certain direction, then all was well, and the hunters would go happily forward. But if the birds acted in the opposite way, nothing in the world could persuade the chief to go on. Evidently the birds gave their permission to bring the travelers home, for in spite of many halts, the savages still moved forward.

They had been struggling for some miles through underbrush and prickly rattan and the white men's clothes were torn and their hands scratched. Now, however, they came upon a well-beaten path, winding up the mountainside, and it proved a great relief to the weary travelers. But here occurred another delay. The savages all stopped, and the chief approached Mackay and spoke to him through the interpreter. Would the white man join him in a head-hunting expedition, was his modest request. There were some Chinese not so far below them, cutting out rattan, and he was sure they could secure one or more heads. He shook the big net head-bag that hung over his shoulder and grinned savagely as he made his proposal. If the white men and their party would come at the enemy from one side, he and his men would attack them from the other, he said, and they would be sure to get them all. The incongruity of a Christian missionary being invited on a head-hunt struck Captain Bax as rather funny in spite of its gruesomeness. This was a delicate situation to handle, but Mackay put a bold front on it. He answered indignantly that he and his friend had come in peace to visit the chief, and that he was neither kind nor honorable in trying to get his visitors to fight his battles.

The interpreter translated and for a moment several pairs of savage eyes gleamed angrily at the bold white man. But second thoughts proved calmer. After another council the savages moved on.

They were now at the top of a range, and every one was ordered to halt and remain silent. Mackay thought that advice was again to be asked of some troublesome little birds, but instead the savages raised a peculiar long-drawn shout. It was answered at once from the opposite mountain-top, and immediately the whole party moved on down the slope.

Here was the same lovely tangle of vines and ferns and beautiful flowers. Monkeys sported in the trees and chattered and scolded the intruders. Down one range and up another they scrambled and at last they came upon the village of the head-hunters.

It lay in a valley in an open space where the forest trees had been cleared away. It consisted of some half-dozen houses or huts made of bamboo or wickerwork, and the place seemed literally swarming with women and children and noisy yelping dogs. But even these could not account for the terrible din that seemed to fill the valley. Such unearthly yells and screeches the white men had never heard before.

"What is it?" asked Captain Bax. "Has the whole village gone mad?"

Mackay turned to one of his guides, and the man explained that the noise came from a village a little farther down the valley. A young hunter had returned with a Chinaman's head, and his friends were rejoicing over it. The merrymaking sounded to the visitors more like the howling of a pack of fiends, for it bore no resemblance to any human sounds they had ever heard.

Fortunately they were invited to stop at the nearer village and were not compelled to take part in the horrible celebration. They were taken at once to the chief's house. It was the best in the village, and boasted of a floor, made of rattan ropes half an inch thick. All along the outside wall, under the eaves, hung a row of gruesome ornaments, heads of the boar and deer and other wild animals killed in the chase, and here and there mingled with them the skulls of Chinamen. The house held one large room, and, as it was a cold evening, a fire burned at either end of it. At one end the men stood chatting, at the other the women squatted. The visitors were invited to sit by the men's fire. There were several beds along the wall, two of which were offered to the strangers. But they were not prepared to remain for the night, and had decided to start back before the shadows fell.

The whole village came to the chief's house and crowded round the newcomers, men first, women and children on the outskirts, and dogs still farther back. Several men came forward and claimed Mackay as a friend. They touched their own breasts and then his, in salutation, grinning in a most friendly manner. The young missionary was at first puzzled, then smiled delightedly. They were some of the poor fellows to whom he had given quinine the evening before in the valley.

This greeting seemed to encourage the others. They became more friendly and suddenly one man who had been circling round the visitors touched the back of Mackay's head and exclaimed, "They do not wear the cue! They are our kinsmen." From that moment they were treated with far greater kindness, and on several other visits that Mackay made to the head-hunters, they always spoke with interest of him as kinsman.

But all danger was not over. The savages were still suspicious, and at any moment the newcomers might excite them. So they decided to start back at once, while every one was in a friendly mood. They made presents to the chief and some of his leading men; and left with expressions of good-will on both sides.

By evening they had reached the valley where they had first met the savages and here they prepared to spend the night. They had no sooner kindled their fires than from the darkness on every side shadowy forms silently emerged—the savages come to visit them! They glided out of the black forest into the ring of firelight and squatted upon the ground until fully five hundred dusky faces looked out at the travelers from the gloom. It was rather an unpleasant situation, there in the depths of the forest, but Mackay turned it to good account. First he and Captain Bax made presents to the head-men and they were as pleased as children to receive the gay ornaments and bright cloth the travelers gave them. And then Mackay called their interpreter to his side and they stood up together, facing the crowd. Speaking through his interpreter, the missionary said he wished to tell them a story. These mountain savages were veritable children in their love for a story, as they were in so many other ways, and their eyes gleamed with delight.

It was a wonderful story he told them, the like of which they had never heard before. It was about the great God, who had made the earth and the people on it, and was the Father of them all. He told how God loved everybody, because they were his children. Chinese, white men beyond the sea like himself and Captain Bax, the people of the mountains,—all were God's children. And so all men were brothers, and should love God their Father and each other. And because God loved his children so, he sent his Son, Jesus Christ, to live among men and to die for them. He told the story simply and beautifully, just as he would to little children, and these children of the forest listened and their savage eyes grew less fierce as they heard for the first time of the story of the Savior.

The next day, after a toilsome journey, the travelers reached the plain below. They had made their dangerous trip and had escaped the head-hunters, but as fierce an enemy was lying in wait for both, an enemy that in Formosa devours native and foreigner alike. Captain Bax was the first to be attacked. All day, as they descended the mountain, the rain came down in torrents, a real Formosan rain that is like the floodgates opening. The travelers were drenched and chilly, and just as they emerged from the forest Captain Bax succumbed to the enemy. Malaria had smitten him.

Shaking with chills and then burning with fever, he was placed in a sedan-chair and carried the remainder of the way, three days' journey, to the coast, where the medical attendants on board his ship cured him. Mackay was feeling desperately ill all the way across the plain, but with his usual determination he refused to give in until he almost staggered across the threshold of his home.

The house had been closed in his absence. It was now damp and chilly and everything was covered with mold. He lay down in his bed, alternately shivering with cold and burning with fever. In the next room A

Hoa, who had gone to bed also, heard his teeth chattering and came to him at once. It was a terrible thing to the young fellow to see his dauntless Kai Bok-su overcome by any kind of force. It seemed impossible that he who had cured so many should become a victim himself. A Hoa proved a kind nurse. He stayed by the bedside all night, doing everything in his power to allay the fever. His efforts proved successful, and in a few days the patient was well. But never again was he quite free from the dreaded disease, and all the rest of his life he was subject to the most violent attacks of malaria, a terrible memento by which he was always to remember his first visit to the head-hunters.

CITIES CAPTURED AND FORTS BUILT

CHAPTER VIII

CITIES CAPTURED AND FORTS BUILT

UP the river to Go-ko-khi! That was always a joy, and whenever Mackay could take a day from his many duties, with A Hoa and one or more other students, he would go up and visit old Thah-so and the kindly people of this little village.

One day, after they had preached in the empty granary and the rain had come in, Mr. Tan, the headman, walked up the village street with them, and he made them an offer. They might have the plot of ground opposite his house for a chapel-site. This was grand news. A chapel in north Formosa! Mackay could hardly believe it, but it seemed that there really was to be one. There were many Christians in Go-ko-khi now, and each one was ready for work. Some collected stones, others prepared sun-dried bricks, others dug the foundation, and the first church in north Formosa was commenced.

Now Go-ko-khi was, unfortunately, near the great city of Bang-kah. This was the most hostile and wicked place in all that country, and A Hoa and Mackay had been stoned out of it on their visit there. The people in Bang-kah learned of the new church building, and one day, when the brick walls were about three feet high, there arose a tramp of feet, beating of drums, and loud shouts, and up marched a detachment of soldiers sent with orders from the prefect of Bang-kah to stop the building of the chapel. Their officers went straight to the house of the headman with his commands. Mr. Tan was six feet two and he rose to his full height and towered above his visitor majestically. The "mayor" of Go-ko-khi was a Christian now, and on the wall of his house was pasted a large sheet of paper with the ten commandments printed on it. He pointed to this and said: "I am determined to abide by these." The officer was taken aback. He was scarcely prepared to defy the headman, and he went away to stir up the villagers. But everywhere the soldiers met with opposition. There seemed no one who would take their part. The officer knew he and his men were scarcely within their rights in what they were doing; so, fearing trouble, he marched back to the city, reporting there that the black-bearded barbarian had bewitched the villagers with some magic art.

The prefect of Bang-kah next sent a message to the British consul. The missionary was building a fort at Go-ko-khi, he declared in great alarm, and would probably bring guns up the river at night. He was a very bad man indeed, and if the British consul desired peace he should stop this wicked Kai Bok-su at once. And the British consul down in his old Dutch fort at Tamsui laughed heartily over the letter, knowing all about Kai Bok-su and the sort of fort he was building.

So, in spite of all opposition, the little church rose steadily up and up until it was crowned with a tiled roof and was ready for the worshipers.

That was a great day for north Formosa and its young missionary, the day the first church was opened. The place was packed to the doors, and many stood outside listening at the windows. And of that crowd one hundred and fifty arose and declared that from henceforth they would cast away their idols and worship only the one and true God. Standing up there in his first pulpit and looking down upon the crowd of upturned faces, and seeing the new light in them which the blessed good news of Jesus and his love had brought, Kai Bok-su's heart swelled with joy.

He stayed with them some time after this, for, though so many people had become Christians, they were like little children and needed much careful teaching. Especially they must learn how to live as Jesus Christ would have his followers live. Many heathen as well as the Christians came to his meetings and listened eagerly. At first the people found it almost impossible to sit quiet and still during a service. They had never been accustomed to such a task, and some of the missionary's experiences were very funny. When they had sung a hymn and had settled down to listen to the address, the preacher would no sooner start than out would come one long pipe after another, pieces of flint would strike on steel, and in a few minutes the smoke would begin to ascend. Mackay would pause and gently tell them that as this was a Christian service they must not do anything that might disturb it. They were anxious to do just as he bade, so the pipes would disappear, and nodding their heads politely they would say, "Oh, yes, we must be quiet; oh, yes, indeed."

One day when the congregation was very still and their young pastor was speaking earnest words to them, one man less attentive than the others happened to glance out of the window. Instantly he sprang to his feet shouting, "Buffaloes in the rice-fields! Buffaloes in the rice-fields!" and away he went with a good fraction of the congregation helter-skelter at his heels.

The missionary spoke again upon the necessity of quiet, and his hearers nodded agreeably and murmured, "Yes, yes, we must be quiet."

They were very good for the next few minutes and the minister had reached a very important point in his address, when there was a great disturbance at the door. An old woman came hobbling up on her small feet and poking her head in at the church door screamed, "My pig has gone! Pig has gone!" and away went another portion of the congregation to help find the truant porker.

But, in spite of many interruptions, the congregation at Go-ko-khi learned much of the beautiful truth of their new religion. Their indulgent pastor never blamed his restless hearers, but before the church was two months old he had trained them so well that there was not a more orderly and attentive congregation even in his own Christian Canada than that which gathered in the first chapel in north Formosa.

But the day came at last when he had to leave them, and the question was who should be left over them. The answer seemed very plain,—A Hoa. The first convert placed as pastor over the first church! It was very fitting. Some months before, down in Tamsui, when A Hoa had been baptized and had taken his first communion, he had vowed to give his life more fully to his Master's service. So here was his field of labor, and here he began his work. He was so utterly sincere and lovable, so bright and jovial, so firm of purpose and yet so kindly, that he was soon beloved by all the Christians and respected by the heathen. And one of his greatest helpers was widow Thah-so, who had been instrumental in bringing the missionary with his glad tidings to her village.

Mackay missed A Hoa sorely at first, but he had his other students about him, and often when bent upon a long journey would send for his first convert, and together they would travel here and there over the island, making new recruits everywhere for the army of their great Captain.

The little church at Go-ko-khi was but the first of many. Like the hepaticas that used to peep forth in the missionary's home

[illegible]

[illegible]

[illegible]

[illegible]

[illegible]

[illegible]

[illegible]

gether and declared they must build a chapel for the worship of the true God.

So, close by the riverside, in a most picturesque spot, the walls of the second chapel of north Formosa began to rise. It was not without opposition of course. One rabid idol-worshiper stopped before the half-finished building with its busy workmen, and, picking up a large stone, declared that he would smash the head of the black-bearded barbarian if the work was not stopped that moment. Needless to say, the missionary, standing within a good stone's throw of his enemy, ordered the workers to continue. George Mackay was not to be stopped by all the stones in north Formosa.

This stone was never thrown, however, and at last the chapel was finished. Once more a preacher was ready to be its pastor. Tan He, a young man who had been studying earnestly under his leader for some time, was placed over this second congregation, and once more there blossomed out a sure sign that the spring had indeed come to north Formosa.

Tek-chham, a walled city of over forty thousand inhabitants, was the next place to be attacked by this little army of the King's soldiers. The first visit of the missionary caused a riot, but before long Tek-chham had a chapel with some of the rioters for its best members, and a once proud graduate and worshiper of Confucius installed in it as its pastor.

Ten miles from Tek-chham stood a little village called Geh-bai. The missionary-soldiers visited it, and to their delight found a church building ready for them. It was quite a wonderful place, capable of holding fully a thousand people without much crowding. Its roof was the boughs of the great banyan tree; its one pillar the trunk, and its walls the branches that bent down to enter the ground and take root. It made a delightful shelter from the broiling sun. And here Kai Bok-su preached. But a banyan does not give perfect shelter in all kinds of weather, so when a number of people had declared themselves followers of the Lord Jesus, a large house was rented and fitted up as a chapel, with another native pastor over it.

Away over at Kelung a church was founded through a man who had carried the gospel home from one of the missionary's sermons. Here and there the hepaticas were springing up. From all sides came invitations to preach the great news of the true God, and the young missionary gave himself scarcely time to eat or sleep. He worked like a giant himself, and he inspired the same spirit in the students that accompanied him. He was like a Napoleon among his soldiers. Wherever he went they would go, even though it would surely mean abuse and might mean death. And, wherever they went, they brought such a wonderful, glad change to people's hearts that they were like slave-liberators setting captives free.

The most lawless and dangerous region in all north Formosa was that surrounding the small town of Sa-kak-eng. In the mountains near by lived a band of robbers who kept the people in a constant state of dread by their terrible deeds of plunder and murder. Sometimes the frightened townspeople would help the highwaymen just to gain their good-will, and such treatment only made them bolder. Bands of them would even come down into the town and march through the streets, frightening every one into flight. They would shout and sing, and their favorite song was one that showed how little they cared for the laws of the land.

> You trust the mandarins,
> We trust the mountains.

So the song went, and when the missionary heard it first he could not help confessing that after all it was a sorry job trusting the mandarins for protection.

The first time he visited the place with A Hoa they were stoned and driven out. But the missionaries came back, and at last were allowed to preach. And then converts came and a church was established. The robber bands received no more assistance from the people, and were soon scattered by the officers of the law. And Sa-kak-eng was in peace because the missionary had come.

But there was one place Mackay had so far scarcely dared to enter. Even the robber-infested Sa-kak-eng would yield, but Bang-kah defied all efforts. To the missionary it was the Gibraltar of heathen Formosa, and he longed to storm it. North, south, east, and west of this great wicked city churches had been planted, some only within a few miles of its walls. But Bang-kah still stood frowning and unyielding. It had always been very bitter against outsiders of all kinds. No foreign merchant was allowed to do business in Bang-kah, so no wonder the foreign missionary was driven out.

Mackay had dared to enter the place, being of the sort that would dare anything. It was soon after he had settled in Formosa and A Hoa had accompanied him. The result had been a riot. The streets had immediately filled with a yelling, cursing mob that pelted the two missionaries with stones and rotten eggs and filth, and drove them from the city.

But "Mackay never knew when he was beaten," as a fellow worker of his once said, and though he was taking desperate chances, he went once more inside the walls of Bang-kah. This time he barely escaped with his life, and the city authorities forbade every one, on pain of death, to lease or sell property to him or in any way accommodate the barbarian missionary.

But meanwhile Kai Bok-su was keeping his eye on Bang-kah, and when the territory around had been possessed, he went up to Go-ko-khi and made the daring proposition to A Hoa. Should they go up again and storm the citadel of heathenism? And A Hoa answered promptly and bravely, "Let us go."

So one day early in December, when the winter rains had commenced to pour down, these two marched across the plain and into Bang-kah. By keeping quiet and avoiding the main thoroughfare, they managed to rent a house. It was a low, mean hovel in a dirty, narrow street, but it was inside the forbidden city, and that was something. The two daring young men then procured a large sheet of paper, printed on it in Chinese characters "Jesus' Temple," and pasted it on the door. This announced what they had come for, and they awaited results.

Presently there came the heavy tramp, tramp of feet on the stone pavement. Mackay and A Hoa looked out. A party of soldiers, armed with spears and swords, were returning from camp. They stopped before the hut and read the inscription. They shouted loud threats and tramped away to report the affair to headquarters.

In a short time, with a great noise and tramping, once more soldiers were at the door. Mackay walked out and faced them quietly. The general had given orders that the barbarian must leave this house immediately, the soldier declared in a loud voice. The place belonged to the military authorities.

"Show me your proof," said Mackay calmly. His bold behavior demanded respectful treatment, so the soldier produced the deed for the property.

"I respect your law," said Mackay after he examined it, "and my companion and I will vacate. But I have paid rent for this place, therefore I am entitled to remain for the night. I will not go out until morning."

His firm words and fearless manner had their effect both on the soldiers and the noisy mob waiting for him outside, and the men, muttering angrily, turned away. That night Mackay and A Hoa lay on a dirty grass mat on the mud floor. The place was damp and filthy, but even had it been comfortable they would have had little sleep. For, far into the night, angry soldiers paraded the street. Often their voices rose to a clamor and they would make a rush for the frail door of the little hut. Many times the two young fellows arose, believing their last hour had come. But the long night passed and they found that they were still left untouched.

They rose early and started out. Already a great mob filled the space in front of the house. Even the low roofs of the surrounding houses were covered with people all out early to see the barbarian and his despised companion driven from Bang-kah, and perhaps have the added pleasure of witnessing their death.

The two walked bravely down the street. Curses were showered upon them from all sides; broken tiles, stones, and filth were thrown at them, but they moved on steadily. The mob hampered them so that they were hours walking the short distance to the river. Here they entered a boat and went down a few miles to a point where a chapel stood, and where some of Mackay's students awaited them.

But the man who "did not know when he was beaten" had not turned his back on the enemy. He gathered the group of students around him in the little room attached to the chapel. Here they all knelt and the young missionary laid their trouble before the great Captain who had said, "All power is given unto me." "Give us an entrance to Bang-kah," was the burden of the missionary's prayer. They arose from their knees, and he turned to A Hoa with that quick challenging movement his students had learned to know so well.

"Come," he said, "we are going back to Bang-kah."

And A Hoa, whose habit it was to walk into all danger with a smile, answered with all his heart:

"It is well, Kai Bok-su; we go back to Bang-kah."

And straight back to this Gibraltar the little army of two marched. It was quite dark by the time they entered. A Formosan city is not the blaze of electricity to which Westerners are accustomed, and only here and there in the narrow streets shone a dim light. The travelers stumbled along, scarcely knowing whither they were going. As they turned a dark corner and plunged into another black street they met an old man hobbling with the aid of a staff over the uneven stones of the pavement. Mackay spoke to him politely and asked if he could tell him of any one who would rent a house. "We want to do mission work," he added, feeling that he must not get anything under false pretenses.

The old man nodded. "Yes, I can rent you

my place," he answered readily. "Come with me."

Full of amazement and gratitude the two adventurers groped their way after him, stumbling over stones and heaps of rubbish. They could not help realizing, as they got farther into the city, that should the old man prove false and give an alarm the whole murderous populace of that district would be around them instantly like a swarm of hornets. But whether he was leading them into a trap or not their only course was to follow.

At last he paused at a low door opening into the back part of a house. The old man lighted a lamp, a pith wick in a saucer of peanut oil, and the visitors looked around. The room was damp and dirty and infested with the crawling creatures that fairly swarm in the Chinese houses of the lower order. Rain dripped from the low ceiling on the mud floor, and the meager furniture was dirty and sticky.

But the two young men who had found it were delighted. They felt like the advance guard of an army that has taken the enemy's first outpost. They were established in Bang-kah! They set to work at once to draw out a rental paper. A Hoa sat at the table and wrote it out so that they might be within the law which said that no foreigner must hold property in Bang-kah. When the paper was signed and the money paid, the old man crept stealthily away. He had his money, but he was too wary to let his fellow citizens find how he had earned it.

As soon as morning came the little army in the midst of the hostile camp hoisted its banner. When the citizens of Bang-kah awoke, they found on the door of the hut the hated sign, in large Chinese characters, "Jesus' Temple."

In less than an hour the street in front of it was thronged with a shouting crowd. Before the day was past the news spread, and the whole city was in an uproar. By the next afternoon the excitement had reached white heat, and a wild crowd of men came roaring down the street. They hurled themselves at the little house where the missionaries were waiting and literally tore it to splinters. The screams of rage and triumph were so horrible that they reminded Mackay of the savage yells of the head-hunters.

When the mob leaped upon the roof and tore it off, the two hunted men slipped out through a side door, and across the street into an inn. The crowd instantly attacked it, smashing doors, ripping the tiles off the roof, and uttering such bloodthirsty howls that they resembled wild beasts far more than human beings. The landlord ordered the missionaries out to where the mob was waiting to tear them limb from limb.

It was an awful moment. To go out was instant death, to remain merely put off the end a few moments. Mackay, knowing his source of help, sent up a desperate prayer to his Father in heaven.

Suddenly there was a strange lull in the street outside. The yells ceased, the crashing of tiles stopped. The door opened, and there in his sedan-chair of state surrounded by his bodyguard, appeared the Chinese mandarin. And just behind him—blessed sight to the eyes of Kai Bok-su—Mr. Scott, the British consul of Tamsui!

Without a word the two British-born clasped hands. It was not an occasion for words. There was immediately a council of war. The mandarin urged the British consul to send the missionary out of the city.

"I have no authority to give such an order," retorted Mr. Scott quickly. "On the other hand you must protect him while he is here. He is a British subject."

Mackay's heart swelled with pride. And he thanked God that his Empire had such a worthy representative.

Having again impressed upon the mandarin that the missionary must be protected or there would be trouble, Mr. Scott set off for his home. Mackay accompanied him to the city gate. Then he turned and walked back through the muttering crowds straight to the inn he had left. He stopped occasionally to pull a tooth or give medicine for malaria, for even in Bang-kah he had a few friends.

The mandarin was now as much afraid of

the missionary as if he had been the plague. He knew he dared not allow him to be touched, and he also knew he had very little power over a mob. He was responsible, too, to men in higher office, for the control of the people, and would be severely punished if there was a riot. He was indeed in a very bad way when he heard that the troublesome missionary had come back, and he followed him to the inn to try to induce him to leave.

He found Mackay with A Hoa, quietly seated in their room. First he commanded, then he tried to bribe, and then he even descended to beg the "foreign devil" to leave the city. But Mackay was immovable.

"I cannot leave," he said, touched by the man's distress. "I cannot quit this city until I have preached the gospel here." He held up his forceps and his Bible. "See! I use these to relieve pain of the body, and this gives relief from sin,—the disease of the soul. I cannot go until I have given your people the benefit of them."

The mandarin went away enraged and baffled. He could not persuade the man to go; he dared not drive him out. He left a squad of soldiers to guard the place, however, remembering the British consul's warning.

In a few days the excitement subsided. People became accustomed to seeing the barbarian teacher and his companion go about the streets. Many were relieved of much pain by him too, and a large number listened with some interest to the new doctrine he taught concerning one God.

He had been there a week when some prominent citizens came to him with a polite offer. They would give him free a piece of ground outside the city on which to build a church. Kai Bok-su's flashing black eyes at once saw the bribe. They wanted to coax him out when they could not drive him. He refused politely but firmly.

"I own that property," he declared, pointing to the heap of ruins into which his house had been turned, "and there I will build a church."

They did everything in their power to prevent him, but one day, many months after, right on the site where they had literally torn the roof from above him, arose a pretty little stone church, and that was the beginning of great things in Bang-kah.

And so Gibraltar was taken,—taken by an army of two,—a Canadian missionary and a Chinese soldier of the King, for behind them stood all the army of the Lord of hosts, and He led them to victory!

OTHER CONQUESTS

CHAPTER IX

OTHER CONQUESTS.

AWAY over on the east of the island ran a range of beautiful mountains. And between these mountains and the sea stretched a low rice plain. Here lived many Pe-po-hoan,—"Barbarians of the plain." Mackay had never visited this place, for the Kap-tsu-lan plain, as it was called, was very hard to reach on account of the mountains; but this only made the dauntless missionary all the more anxious to visit it.

So one day he suggested to his students, as they studied in his house on the bluff, that they make a journey to tell the people of Kap-tsu-lan the story of Jesus. Of course, the young fellows were delighted. To go off with Kai Bok-su was merely transferring their school from his house to the big beautiful outdoors. For he always taught them by the way, and besides they were all eager to go with him and help spread the good news that had made such a difference in their lives. So when Kai Bok-su piled his books upon a shelf and said, "Let us go to Kap-tsu-lan," the young fellows ran and made their preparations joyfully. A Hoa was in Tamsui at the time, and Mackay suggested that he come too, for a trip without A Hoa was robbed of half its enjoyment.

Mackay had just recovered from one of those violent attacks of malaria from which he suffered so often now, and he was still looking pale and weak. So Sun-a, a bright young student-lad, came to the study door with the suggestion, "Let us take Lu-a for Kai Bok-su to ride."

There was a laugh from the other students and an indulgent smile from Kai Bok-su himself. Lu-a was a small, rather stubborn-looking donkey with meek eyes and a little rat tail. He was a present to the missionary from the English commissioner of customs at Tamsui, when that gentleman was leaving the island. Donkeys were commonly used on the mainland of China, and though an animal was scarcely ever ridden in Formosa, horses being almost unknown, the commissioner did not see why his Canadian friend, who was an introducer of so many new things, should not introduce donkey-riding. So he sent him Lu-a as a farewell present and leaving this token of his good-will departed for home.

Up to this time Lu-a had served only as a pet and a joke among the students, and high times they had with him in the grassy field behind the missionary's house when lessons were over. In great glee they brought him round to the door now, "all saddled and bridled" and ready for the trip. The missionary mounted, and Lu-a trotted meekly along the road that wound down the bluff toward Kelung. The students followed in high spirits. The sight of their teacher astride the donkey was such a novel one to them, and Lu-a was such a joke at any time, that they were filled with merriment. All went well until they left the road and turned into a path that led across the buffalo common. At the end of it they came to a ravine about fifteen feet deep. Over this stretched a plank bridge not more than three feet wide. Here Lu-a came to a sudden stop. He had no mind to risk his small but precious body on that shaky structure. His rider bade him "go on," but the command only made Lu-a put back his ears, plant his fore feet well forward and stand stock still. In fact he looked much more settled and immovable than the bridge over which he was being urged. The students gathered round him and petted and coaxed. They called him "Good Lu-a" and "Honorable Lu-a" and every other flattering title calculated to move his donkeyship, but Lu-a flattened his ears back so he could not hear and would not move. So Mackay dismounted and tried the plan of pulling him forward by the bridle while some of the boys pushed him from behind. Lu-a resented this treatment, especially that from the rear, and up went his heels, scattering students in every direction; and to discomfit the enemy in front he opened his mouth and gave forth such loud resonant brays that the ravine fairly rang with his music.

A balking donkey is rather amusing to boys of any country, but to these Formosan lads who had had no experience with one the sound of Lu-a's harsh voice and the sight of his flying heels brought convulsions of merriment. "He's pounding rice! He's pounding rice!" shouted the wag of the party, and his companions flung themselves upon the grass and rolled about laughing themselves sick.

With his followers rendered helpless and his steed continuing stubborn, Mackay saw the struggle was useless. He could not compete alone with Lu-a's firmness, so he gave orders that the obstinate little obstructer of their journey be trotted back to his pasture.

"And to think that any one of us might have carried the little rascal over!" he cried as he watched the donkey meekly depart. His students looked at the little beast with something like respect. Lu-a had beaten the dauntless Kai Bok-su who had never before been beaten by anything. He was indeed a marvelous donkey!

So the journey to the Kap-tsu-lan plain was made on foot. It was a very wearisome one and often dangerous. The mountain paths were steep and difficult and the travelers knew that often the head-hunters lurked near. But the way was wonderfully beautiful nevertheless. Standing on a mountain height one morning and looking away down over wooded hills and valleys and the lake-like terraces of the rice-fields, Mackay repeated to his students a line of the old hymn:

> Every prospect pleases and only man is vile.

Around them the stately tree-fern lifted its lovely fronds and the orchids dotted the green earth like a flock of gorgeous butterflies just settled. Tropical birds of brilliant plumage flashed among the trees. Beside them a great tree raised itself, fairly covered with morning-glories, and over at their right a mountainside gleamed like snow in the sunlight, clothed from top to bottom with white lilies.

But the way had its dangers as well as its beauties. They were passing the mouth of a ravine when they were stopped by yells and screams of terror coming from farther up the mountainside. In a few minutes a Chinaman darted out of the woods toward them. His face was distorted with terror and he could scarcely get breath to tell his horrible story. He and his four companions had been chipping the camphor trees up in the woods; suddenly the armed savages had leaped out upon them and he alone of the five had escaped.

At last they left the dangerous mountain and came down into the Kap-tsu-lan plain. On every side was rice-field after rice-field, with the water pouring from one terrace to another. The plain was low and damp and the paths and roads lay deep in mud. They had a long toilsome walk between the rice-fields until they came to the first village of these barbarians of the plain. It was very much like a Chinese village,—dirty, noisy, and swarming with wild-looking children and wolfish dogs.

The visitors were received with the utmost disdain. The Chinese students were of course well known, for these aborigines had long ago adopted their customs and language. But the Chinese visitors were in company with the foreigners, and all foreigners were outcaste in this eastern plain. The men shouted the familiar "foreign devil" and walked contemptuously away. The dirty women and children fled into their grass huts and set the dogs upon the strangers. They tried by all sorts of kindnesses to gain a hearing, but all to no effect. So they gave it up, and plodded through the mud and water a mile farther on to the next village. But village number two received them in exactly the same way. Only rough words and the barks of cruel dogs met them. The next village was no better, the fourth a little worse. And so on they went up and down the Kap-tsu-lan plain, sleeping at night in some poor empty hut or in the shadow of a rice strawstack, eating their meals of cold rice and buffalo-meat by the wayside, and being driven from village to village, and receiving never a word of welcome.

And all through those wearisome days the young men looked at their leader in vain for any smallest sign of discouragement or inclination to retreat. There was no slightest look of dismay on the face of Kai Bok-su, for how was it possible for a man who did not know when he was beaten to feel discouraged? So still undaunted in the face of defeat, he led them here and there over the plain, hoping that some one would surely relent and give them a hearing.

One night, footsore and worn out, they slept on the damp mud floor of a miserable hut where the rain dripped in upon their faces. In the morning prospects looked rather discouraging to the younger members of the party. They were wet and cold and weary, and there seemed no use in going again and again to a village only to be turned away. But Kai Bok-su's mouth was as firm as ever, and his dark eyes flashed resolutely, as once more he gave the order to march. It was a lovely morning, the sun was rising gloriously out of the sea and the heavy mists were melting from above the little rice-fields. Here and there fairy lakes gleamed out from the rosy haze that rolled back toward the mountains. They walked along the shore in the pink dawn-light and marched up toward a fishing village. They had visited it before and had been driven away, but Kai Bok-su was determined to try again. They were surprised as they came nearer to see three men come out to meet them with a friendly expression on their faces.

The foremost was an old man who had been nicknamed "Black-face," because of his dark skin. The second was a middle-aged man, and the third was a young fellow about the age of the students. They saluted the travelers pleasantly, and the old man addressed the missionary.

"You have been going through and through our plain and no one has received you," he said politely. "Come to our village, and we will now be ready to listen to you."

The door of Kap-tsu-lan had opened at last! The missionary's eyes gleamed with joy and gratitude as he accepted the invitation. The delegation led the visitors straight to the house of the headman. For the Pe-po-hoan governed their communities in the Chinese style and had a headman for each village. The missionary party sat down in front of the hut on some large flat stones and talked over the matter with the chief and other important men. And while they talked "Black-face" slipped away. He returned in a few moments with a breakfast of rice and fish for the visitors.

The result of the conference was that the villagers decided to give the barbarian a chance. All he wanted it seemed was to tell of this new Jehovah-religion which he believed, and surely there could be no great harm in listening to him talk.

In the evening the headman with the help of some friends set to work to construct a meeting-house. A tent was erected, made from boat sails. Several flat stones laid at one end and a plank placed upon them made a pulpit. And that was the first church on the Kap-tsu-lan plain! There was a "church bell" too, to call the people to worship. In the village were some huge marine shells with the ends broken off. In the old days these were used by the chiefs as trumpets by which they called their men together whenever they were starting out on the war-path. But now the trumpet-shell was used to call the people to follow the King. Just at dark a man took one, and walking up and down the straggling village street blew loudly—the first "church bell" in east Formosa.

The loud roar brought the villagers flocking down to the tent-church by the shore. For the most part they brought their pews with them. They came hurrying out of their huts carrying benches, and arranging them in rows they seated themselves to listen.

Mackay and the students sang and the people listened eagerly. The Pe-po-hoan by nature were more musical than the Chinese, and the singing delighted them. Then the missionary arose and addressed them. He told clearly and simply why he had come and preached to them of the true God. Afterward the congregation was allowed to ask questions, and they learned much of this God and of his love in his Son Jesus Christ.

The wonder of the great news shone in the eyes upturned to the preacher. In the gloom of the half-lighted tent their dark faces took on a new expression of half-wondering hope. Could it be possible that this was true? Their poor, benighted minds had always been held in terror of their gods and of the evil spirits that forever haunted their footsteps. Could it be possible that God was a great Father who loved his children? They asked so many eager questions, and the story of Jesus Christ had to be told over and over so many times, that before this first church service ended a gray gleam of dawn was spreading out over the Pacific.

It was only the next day that these newly-awakened people decided that they must have a church building. And they went to work to get one in a way that might have shamed a congregation of people in a Christian land. This new wonderful hope that had been raised in their hearts by the knowledge that God loved them set them to work with glad energy. Kai Bok-su and his men still preached and prayed and sang and taught in the crazy old wind-flapped tent by the seashore, and the people listened eagerly, and then, when services were over, every one,—preacher, assistants, and congregation,—set bravely to work to build a church. Brave they certainly had to be, for at the very beginning they had to risk their lives for their chapel. A party sailed down the coast and entered savage territory for the poles to construct the building. They were attacked and one or two were badly wounded, though they managed to escape. But they were quite ready to go back and fight again had it been necessary. Then they made the bricks for the walls. Rice chaff mixed with clay were the materials, and the Kap-tsu-lan plain had an abundance of both. The roof was made of grass, the floor of hard dried earth, and a platform of the same at one end served as a pulpit.

When the little chapel was finished, every evening the big shell rang out its summons through the village; and out from every house came the people and swarmed into the chapel to hear Kai Bok-su explain more of the wonders of God and his Son Jesus Christ.

Mackay's home during this period was a musty little room in a damp mud-walled hut; and here every day he received donations of idols, ancestral tablets, and all sorts of things belonging to idol-worship. He was requested to burn them, and often in the mornings he dried his damp clothes and moldy boots at a fire made from heathen idols.

For eight weeks the missionary party remained in this place, preaching, teaching, and working among the people. It was a mystery to the students how their teacher found time for the great amount of Bible study and prayer which he managed to get. He surely worked as never man worked before. Late at night, long after every one else was in bed, he would be bending over his Bible, beside his peanut-oil lamp, and early in the morning before the stars had disappeared he was up and at work again. Four hours' sleep was all his restless, active mind could endure, and with that he could do work that would have killed any ordinary man.

One evening some new faces looked up at him from his congregation in the little brick church. When the last hymn was sung the missionary stepped down from his pulpit and spoke to the strangers. They explained that they were from the next village. They had heard rumors of this new doctrine, and had been sent to find out more about it. They had been charmed with the singing, for that evening over two hundred voices had joined in a ringing praise to the new Jehovah-God. They wanted to hear more, they said, and they wanted to know what it was all about. Would Kai Bok-su and his students deign to visit their village too?

Would he? Why that was just what he was longing to do. He had been driven out of that village by dogs only a few weeks before, but a little thing like that did not matter to a man like Mackay. This village lay but a short distance away, being connected with their own by a path winding here and there between the rice-fields. Early the next evening Mackay formed a procession. He placed himself at its head, with A Hoa at his side. The students came next, and then the converts in a double row. And thus they marched slowly along the pathway singing as they went. It was a stirring sight. On either side the waving fields of rice, behind them the gleam of the blue ocean, before them the great towering mountains clothed in green. Above them shone the clear dazzling sky of a tropical evening. And on wound the long procession of Christians in a heathen land, and from them arose the glorious words:

O thou, my soul, bless God the Lord,
  And all that in me is
Be stirred up his holy name
  To magnify and bless.

And the heathen in the rice-fields stopped to gaze at the strange sight, and the mountains gave back the echo of that Name which is above every name.

And so, marching to their song, the procession came to the village. Everybody in the place had come out to meet them at the first sound of the singing. And now they stood staring, the men in a group by themselves, the women and children in the background, the dogs snarling on the outskirts of the crowd.

The congregation was there ready, and without waiting to find a place of meeting, right out under the clear evening skies, the young missionary told once more the great story of God and his love as shown through Jesus Christ. The message took the village by storm. It was like water to thirsty souls. The next day five hundred of them brought their idols to the missionary to be burned.

And now Mackay went up and down the Kap-tsu-lan plain from village to village as he had done before, but this time it was a triumphal march. And everywhere he went throngs threw away their idols and declared themselves followers of the true God.

He was overcome with joy. It was so glorious he wished he could stay there the rest of his life and lead these willing people to a higher life. But Tamsui was waiting; Sin-tiam, Bang-kah, Kelung, Go-ko-khi,—they must all be visited; and finally he tore himself away, leaving some of his students to care for these people of Kap-tsu-lan.

But he came back many times, until at last nineteen chapels dotted the plain, and in them nineteen native preachers told the story of Jesus and his love. Sometimes, in later years, when Mackay was with them, tears would roll down the people's faces as they recalled how badly they had used him on his first visit.

It was while on his third visit here that he had a narrow escape from the head-hunters. He was staying at a village called "South Wind Harbor," which was near the border of savage territory. Mackay often walked on the shore in the evening just before the meeting, always with a book in his hand. One night he was strolling along in deep meditation when he noticed some extremely large turtle tracks in the sand. He followed them, for he liked to watch the big clumsy creatures. These green turtles were from four to five feet in length. They would come waddling up from the sea, scratch a hole in the sand with their flippers, lay their eggs, cover them carefully, and with head erect and neck out-thrust waddle back. Mackay was intensely interested in all the animal life of the island and made a study of it whenever he had a chance. He knew the savages killed and ate these turtles, but he supposed he was as yet too near the village to be molested by them. So he followed the tracks and was nearing the edge of the forest, when he heard a shout behind him. As he turned, one of his village friends came running out of his hut waving to him frantically to come back. Thinking some one must be ill, Mackay hurried toward the man, to find that it was he himself who was in danger. The man explained breathlessly that it was the habit of the wily savages to make marks in the sand resembling turtle tracks to lure people into the forest. If Kai

Bok-su had entered the woods, his head would certainly have been lost.

It was always hard to say farewell to Kap-tsu-lan, the people were so warm-hearted, so kind, and so anxious for him to stay. One morning just before leaving after his third visit, Mackay had an experience that brought him the greatest joy.

He had stayed all night at the little fishing village where the first chapel had been built. As usual he was up with the dawn, and after his breakfast of cold boiled rice and pork he walked down to the shore for a farewell look at the village. As he passed along the little crooked street he could see old women sitting on the mud floors of their huts, by the open door, weaving. They were all poor, wrinkled, toothless old folk with faces seamed by years of hard heathen experience. But in their eyes shone a new light, the reflection of the glory that they had seen when the missionary showed them Jesus their Savior. And as they threw their thread their quavering voices crooned the sweet words:

There is a happy land
Far, far away.

And their old weary faces were lighted up with a hope and happiness that had never been there in youth.

Kai Bok-su smiled as he passed their doors and his eyes were misty with tender tears.

Just before him, playing on the sand with "jacks" or tops, just as he had played not so very long ago away back in Canada, were the village boys. And as they played they too were singing, their little piping voices, sweet as birds, thrilling the morning air. And the words they sang were:

Jesus loves me, this I know,
For the Bible tells me so.

They nodded and smiled to Kai Bok-su as he passed. He went down to the shore where the wide Pacific flung long rollers away up the hard-packed sand. The fishermen were going out to sea in the rosy morning light, and as they stood up in their fishing-smacks, and swept their long oars through the surf, they kept time to the motion with singing. And their strong, brave voices rang out above the roar of the breakers:

> I'm not ashamed to own my Lord,
> Or to defend his cause.

And standing there on the sunlit shore the young missionary raised his face to the gleaming blue heavens with an emotion of unutterable joy and thanksgiving. And in that moment he knew what was that glory for which he had so vaguely longed in childish years. It was the glory of work accomplished for his Master's sake, and he was realizing it to the full.

REENFORCEMENTS

CHAPTER X

REENFORCEMENTS

SOME of Mackay's happiest days were spent with his students. He was such a wonder of a man for work himself that he inspired every one else to do his best, so the young men made rapid strides with their lessons. No matter how busy he was, and he was surely one of the busiest men that ever lived, he somehow found time for them.

Sometimes in his house, sometimes on the road, by the seashore, under a banyan tree, here and there and everywhere, the missionary and his pupils held their classes. If he went on a journey, they accompanied him and studied by the way. And it was a familiar sight on north Formosan roads or field paths to see Mackay, always with his book in one hand and his big ebony stick under his arm, walking along surrounded by a group of young men.

Sometimes there were as many as twenty in the student-band, but somewhere in the country a new church would open, and the brightest of the class would be called away to be its minister. But just as often a young Christian would come to the missionary and ask if he too might not be trained to preach the gospel of Jesus Christ.

Whether at home or abroad, pupils and teacher had to resort to all sorts of means to get away for an uninterrupted hour together. For Kai Bok-su was always in demand to visit the sick or sad or troubled.

There was a little kitchen separate from the house on the bluff, and over this Mackay with his students built a second story. And here they would often slip away for a little quiet time together. One night, about eleven o'clock, Mackay was here alone poring over his books. The young men had gone home to bed except two or three who were in the kitchen below. Some papers had been dropped over a pipe-hole in the floor of the room where Mackay was studying, and for some time he had been disturbed by a rustling among them. At last without looking up, he called to his boys below: "I think there are rats up here among my papers!"

Koa Kau, one of the younger of the students, ran lightly up the stairs to give battle to the intruders. What was his horror when he saw fully three feet of a monster serpent sticking up through the pipe-hole and waving its horrible head in the air just a little distance from Kai Bok-su's chair.

The boy gave a shout, darted down the stair, and with a sharp stick, pinned the body of the snake to the wall below. The creature became terribly violent, but Koa Kau held on valiantly and Mackay seized an old Chinese spear that happened to be in the room above and pierced the serpent through the head. They pulled its dead body down into the kitchen below and spread it out. It measured nine feet. The students would not rest until it was buried, and the remembrance of the horrible creature's visit for some time spoiled the charm of the little upper room.

The rocks at Kelung harbor were another

favorite spot for this little traveling university to hold its classes. Sometimes they would take their dinner and row out in a little sampan to the rocks outside the harbor and there, undisturbed, they would study the whole day long.

They always began the day's work with a prayer and a hymn of praise, and no matter what subjects they might study, most of the time was spent on the greatest of books. After a hard morning's work each one would gather sticks, make a fire, and they would have their dinner of vegetables, rice, and pork or buffalo-meat. Then there were oysters, taken fresh off the rocks, to add to their bill of fare.

At five in the afternoon, when the strain of study was beginning to tell, they would vary the program. One or two of the boys would take a plunge into the sea and bring up a subject for study,—a shell, some living coral, sea-weed, sea-urchins, or some such treasure. They would examine it, and Kai Bok-su, always delighted when on a scientific subject, would give them a lesson in natural history. And he saw with joy how the wonders of the sea and land opened these young men's minds to understand what a great and wonderful God was theirs, who had made "the heaven and the earth and the sea, and all that in them is."

When they visited a chapel in the country, they had a daily program which they tried hard to follow. They studied until four o'clock every afternoon and all were trained in speaking and preaching. After four they made visits together to Christians or heathen, speaking always a word for their Master. Every evening a public service was held at which Mackay preached. These sermons were an important part of the young men's training, for he always treated the gospel in a new way. A Hoa, who was Mackay's companion for the greater part of sixteen years, stated that he had never heard Kai Bok-su preach the same sermon twice.

On the whole the students liked their college best when it was moving. For on the road, while their principal gave much time to the Bible and how to present the gospel, he would enliven their walks by conversing about everything by the way and making it full of interest. The structure of a wayside flower, the geological formation of an overhanging rock, the composition of the soil of the tea plantations, the stars that shone in the sky when night came down upon them; —all these made the traveling college a delight.

Although his days were crammed with work, Mackay found time to make friends among the European population of the island. They all liked and admired him, and many of them tried to help the man who was giving his life and strength so completely to others. They were familiar with his quick, alert figure passing through the streets of Tamsui, with his inevitable book and his big ebony cane. And they would smile and say, "There goes Mackay; he's the busiest man in China."[1]

The British consul in the old Dutch fort and the English commissioner of customs proved true and loyal friends. The repre-

[1] See page 290. Formosa becomes Japanese territory.

sentatives of foreign business firms, too, were always ready to lend him a helping hand where possible. His most useful friends were the foreign medical men. They helped him very much. They not only did all they could for his own recovery when malaria attacked him, but they helped also to cure his patients. Traveling scientists always gave him a visit to get his help and advice. He had friends that were ship-captains, officers, engineers, merchants, and British consuls. Everybody knew the wonderful Kai Bok-su. "Whirlwind Mackay," some of them called him, and they knew and admired him with the true admiration that only a brave man can inspire.

The friends to whom he turned for help of the best kind were the English Presbyterians in south Formosa. They, more than any others, knew his trials and difficulties. They alone could enter with true sympathy into all his triumphs. At one time Dr. Campbell, one of the south Formosan missionaries, paid him a visit. He proved a delightful companion, and together the two made a tour of the mission stations. Dr. Campbell preached wherever they went and was a great inspiration to the people, as well as to the students and to the missionary himself.

One evening, when they were in Kelung, Mackay, with his insatiable desire to use every moment, suggested that they spend ten days without speaking English, so that they might improve their Chinese. Dr. Campbell agreed, and they started their "Chinese only." Next morning from the first early call of "Liong tsong khi lai," "All, all, up come," not one word of their native tongue did they speak. They had a long tramp that morning and there was much to talk about and the conversation was all in Chinese, according to the bargain. Dr. Campbell was ahead, and after an hour's talk he suddenly turned upon his companion: "Mackay!" he exclaimed, "this jabbering in Chinese is ridiculous, and two Scotchmen should have more sense; let us return to our mother tongue." Which advice Mackay gladly followed.

His next visitor was the Rev. Mr. Ritchie

from south Formosa, one of the friends who had first introduced him to his work. Every day of his visit was a joy. With nine of Mackay's students, the two missionaries set out on a trip through the north Formosa mission that lasted many weeks.

But the more pleasant and helpful such companionship was the more alone Mackay felt when it was over. His task was becoming too much for one man. He was wanted on the northern coast, at the southern boundary of his mission field, and away on the Kap-tsu-lan plain all at once. He was crowded day and night with work. What with preaching, dentistry, attending the sick, training his students, and encouraging the new churches, he had enough on his hands for a dozen missionaries.

But now at last the Church at home, in far-away Canada, bestirred herself to help him. They had been hearing something of the wonderful mission in Formosa, but they had heard only hints of it, for Mackay would not confess how he was toiling day and night and how the work had grown until he was not able to overtake it alone. But the Church understood something of his need, and they now sent him the best present they could possibly give,—an assistant. Just three years after Mackay had landed in Formosa, the Rev. J. B. Fraser, M. D., and his wife and little ones arrived. He was a young man, too, vigorous and ready for work. Besides being an ordained minister, he was a physician as well, just exactly what the north Formosan mission needed.

Along with the missionary, the Church had sent funds for a house for him and also one for Mackay. So the poor old Chinese house on the bluff was replaced by a modern, comfortable dwelling, and by its side another was built for the new missionary and his family. One room of Mackay's house was used as a study for his students.

After the houses were built and the new doctor was able to use the language, he began to fill a long-felt want. Mackay had always done a little medical work, and the foreign doctor of Tamsui had been most kind in giving his aid, but a doctor of his own, a missionary doctor, was exactly what Kai Bok-su wanted. Soon the sick began to hear of the wonders the missionary doctor could perform, and they flocked to him to be cured.

It must not be supposed that there were not already doctors in north Formosa. There were many in Tamsui alone, and very indignant they were at this new barbarian's success. But the native doctors were about the worst trouble that the people had to bear. Their medical knowledge, like their religion, was a mixture of ignorance and superstition, and some of their practises would have been inexcusable except for the fact that they themselves knew no better. There were two classes of medical men; those who treated internal diseases and those who professed to cure external maladies. It was hard to judge which class did the more mischief, but perhaps the "inside doctors" killed more of their patients. Dog's flesh was prescribed as a cure for dyspepsia, a chip taken from a coffin and boiled and the water drunk was a remedy for catarrh, and an apology made to the moon was a specific for wind-roughened skin. For the dreaded malaria, the scourge of Formosa, the young Canadian doctor found many and amazing remedies prescribed, some worse than the disease itself. The native doctors believed malaria to be caused by two devils in a patient, one causing the chills, the other the fever. One of the commonest remedies, and one that was quite as sensible as any of the rest, was to tie seven hairs plucked from a black dog around the sick one's wrist.

But when the barbarian doctor opened his dispensary in Tamsui, a new era dawned for the poor sick folk of north Formosa. The work went on wonderfully well and Mackay found so much more time to travel in the country that the gospel spread rapidly.

But just when prospects were looking so fair and every one was happy and hopeful, a sad event darkened the bright outlook of the two missionaries. The young doctor had cured scores of cases, and had brought health and happiness to many homes, but he was powerless to keep death from his own door.

And one day, a sad day for the mission of north Formosa, the mother was called from husband and little ones to her home and her reward in heaven.

So the home on the bluff, the beautiful Christian home, which was a pattern for all the Chinese, was broken up. The young doctor was compelled to leave his patients, and taking his motherless children he returned with them to Canada.

The church at home sent out another helper. The Rev. Kenneth Junor arrived one year later, and once more the work received a fresh impetus. And then, just about two years after Mr. Junor's arrival, Kai Bok-su found an assistant of his own right in Formosa, and one who was destined to become a wonderful help to him. And so one bright day, there was a wedding in the chapel of the old Dutch fort, where the British consul married George Leslie Mackay to a Formosan lady. Tui Chhang Mai, her name had been. She was of a beautiful Christian character and for a long time she had been a great help in the church. But as

Mrs. Mackay she proved a marvelous assistance to her husband.

It had long been a great grief to the missionary that, while the men would come in crowds to his meetings, the poor women had to be left at home. Sometimes in a congregation of two hundred there would be only two or three women. Chinese custom made it impossible for a man missionary to preach to the women. Only a few of the older ones came out. So the mothers of the little children did not hear about Jesus and so could not teach their little ones about him.

But now everything was changed for them. They had a lady-missionary, and one of their own people too. The Mackays went on a wedding-trip through the country. Kai Bok-su walked, as usual, and his wife rode in a sedan-chair. The wedding-trip was really a missionary tour; for they visited all the chapels, and the women came to the meetings in crowds, because they wanted to hear and see the lady who had married Kai Bok-su. Often, after the regular meetings when the men had gone away, the women

Mrs. George L. Mackay

"BUT AS MRS. MACKAY SHE PROVED OF MARVELOUS ASSISTANCE TO HER HUSBAND"

would crowd in and gather round Mrs. Mackay and she would tell them the story of Jesus and his love.

It was a wonderful wedding-journey and it brought a double blessing wherever the two went. Their experiences were not all pleasant. One day they traveled over a sand plain so hot that Mackay's feet were blistered. Another time they were drenched with rain. One afternoon there came up a terrific wind storm. It blew Mrs. Mackay's sedan-chair over and sent her and the carriers flying into the mud by the roadside. At another place they all barely escaped drowning when crossing a stream. But the brave young pair went through it all dauntlessly. The wife had caught something of her husband's great spirit of sacrifice, and he was always the man on fire, utterly forgetful of self.

For two years they worked happily together and at last a great day came to Kai-Bok-su. He had been nearly eight years in Formosa. It was time he came home, the Church in Canada said, for a little rest and to tell the people at home something of his great work.

And so he and his Formosan wife said good-by, amid tears and regrets on all sides, and leaving Mr. Junor in charge with A Hoa to help, they set sail for Canada. It was just a little over seven years since he had settled in that little hut by the river, despised and hated by every one about him; and now he left behind him twenty chapels, each with a native preacher over it, and hundreds of warm friends scattered over all north Formosa.

He was not quite the same Mackay who had stood on the deck of the *America* seven years before. His eyes were as bright and daring as ever and his alert figure as full of energy, but his face showed that his life had been a hard one. And no wonder, for he had endured every kind of hardship and privation in those seven years. He had been mobbed times without number. He had faced death often, and day and night since his first year on the island his footsteps had been dogged by the torturing malaria.

But he was still the great, brave Mackay and his home-coming was like the return of a hero from battle. He went through Canada preaching in the churches, and his words were like a call to arms. He swept over the country like one of his own Formosan winds, carrying all before him. Wherever he preached hearts were touched by his thrilling tales, and purses opened to help in his work. Queen's University made him a Doctor of Divinity; Mrs. Mackay, a lady of Detroit, gave him money enough to build a hospital; and his home county, Oxford, presented him with $6,215 with which to build a college.

He visited his old home and had many long talks of his childhood days with his loved ones. And he was reminded of the big stone in the pasture-field which he was so determined to break. And he thanked his heavenly Father for allowing him to break the great rock of heathenism in north Formosa.

He returned to his mission work more on fire than ever. If he had been received with acclaim in his native land, his Formosan friends' welcome was not less warm. Crowds of converts, all his students who were not too far inland, and among them, Mr. Junor, his face all smiles, were thronging the dock, many of them weeping for joy. It was as if a long-absent father had come back to his children.

The work went forward now by leaps and bounds. Mackay's first thought, after a hurried visit to the chapels and their congregations, was to see that the hospital and college were built.

All day long the sound of the builders could be heard up on the bluff near the missionaries' houses, and in a wonderfully short time there arose two beautiful, stately buildings. Mackay hospital they called one, not for Kai Bok-su—he did not like things named for him—but in memory of the husband of the kind lady who had furnished the money for it. The school for training young men in the ministry was called Oxford College, in honor of the county whose people had made it possible.

"Oxford College Stood just Overlooking the Tamsui River"

Oxford College stood just overlooking the Tamsui river, two hundred feet above its waters. The building was 116 feet long and 67 feet wide, and was built of small red bricks brought from across the Formosa Channel. A wide, airy hall ran down the middle of the building, and was used as a lecture-room. On either side were rooms capable of accommodating fifty students and apartments for two teachers and their families. There were, besides, two smaller lecture-rooms, a museum filled with treasures collected from all over Formosa by Dr. Mackay and his students, a library, a bathroom, and a kitchen.

The grounds about the college and hospital were very beautiful. Nature had given one of the finest situations to be found about Tamsui, and Kai Bok-su did the rest. The climate helped him, for it was no great task to have a luxurious garden in north Formosa. So, in a few years there were magnificent trees and hedges, and always glorious flower beds abloom all the time around the missionary premises.

But all this was not accomplished without great toil, and Kai Bok-su appeared never to rest in those building days. It seemed impossible that one man should work so hard. He was in Tamsui superintending the hospital building to-day, and away off miles in the country preaching to-morrow. He never seemed to get time to eat, and he certainly slept less than his allotted four hours.

A great disappointment was pending, however, and one he saw coming nearer every day. The trying Formosan climate was proving too much for his young assistant, and one sad day he stood on the dock and saw Mr. Junor, pale and weak and broken in health, sail away back to Canada.

But there was always a brave soldier waiting to step into the breach, and the next year Kai Bok-su had the joy of welcoming two new helpers, when the Rev. Mr. Jamieson and his wife came out from Canada and settled in the empty house on the bluff. Yes, and in time there came to his own house other helpers—very little and helpless at first they were—but they soon made the house ring with happy noise and filled the hearts of their parents with joy.

There were two ladies now to lead in the work for girls and women. Their sisters in Canada came to their help too. The young men had a school in Formosa, and why should there not be a school for women and girls? they asked. And so the Women's Foreign Missionary Society of Canada sent to Dr. Mackay money to build one. It took only two months to erect it. It stood just a few rods from Oxford College, and was a fine, airy building. Here a native preacher and his wife took up their abode and with the help of Mrs. Mackay and two other native Christian women they strove to teach the girls of north Formosa how to make beautiful Christian homes.

And now to the two missionaries every prospect seemed bright. The college, the girls' school, the hospital, were all in splendid working order. Mr. and Mrs. Jamieson were giving their best assistance. A Hoa and the other native pastors were working faithfully. God's blessing seemed to be showering down upon the work and on every side were signs of growth. And then, right from this shining sky, there fell a storm of such fierceness that it threatened to wipe out completely the whole north Formosan mission.

UNEXPECTED BOMBARDMENT.

CHAPTER XI

UNEXPECTED BOMBARDMENT

AN enemy's battle-ships off the coast of Formosa! During all the spring rumors of trouble had been coming across the channel from the mainland. France[1] and China had been quarreling over a boundary-line in Tongking. The affair had been settled but not in a way that pleased France. So, without even waiting to declare war, she sent a fleet to the China Sea and bombarded some of her enemy's ports. Formosa, of course, came in for her share of the trouble, and it was early in the summer that the French battle-ships appeared. They hove in sight, sailing down the Formosa Channel or Strait one hot day, and instantly all Formosa was in an uproar of alarm and rage. The rage was greater than the alarm, for

[1] War in 1844.

China cordially despised all peoples beyond her own border, and felt that the barbarians would probably be too feeble to do them any harm. But that the barbarians should dare to approach their coast with a war-vessel! That was a terrible insult, and the fierce indignation of the people knew no bounds. Their rage broke out against all foreigners. They did not distinguish between the missionary from British soil and the French soldiers on their enemy's vessels. They were all barbarians alike, the Chinese declared, and as such were the deadly foe of China. This Kai Bok-su was in league with the French, and the native Christians all over Formosa were in league with him, and all deserved death!

So hard days came for the Christians of north Formosa. Wherever there was a house containing converts, there was riot and disorder. For bands of enraged heathen, armed with knives and swords, would parade the streets about them and threaten all with a violent death the moment the French fired a shot.

In some places near the coast the Christian people dared not leave their houses, and whenever they sent out their children to buy food, often a heathen neighbor would catch them, brandish knives over the terrified little ones' heads and declare they would all be cut to pieces when the barbarian ships came into port.

Every hour of the day and often in the night, letters came from all parts of the country to Dr. Mackay. They were brought by runners who came at great peril of their lives, and were sent by the poor Christians. Each letter told the same tale; the lives and property of all the converts were in grave danger if the enemy did not leave. And they all asked Kai Bok-su to do something to help them.

Now Kai Bok-su was a man with great power and influence both in Formosa and in his far-off Canada, but he had no means of bringing that power to bear on the French. And indeed his own life was in as great danger as any one's.

He wrote to the Christians comforting

them and enthusing them with his own spirit. He bade them all be brave, and no matter what came, danger or torture or death itself, they must be true to Jesus Christ. He went about his work in the college or hospital just as usual, though he knew that any day the angry mob from the town below might come raging up to destroy and kill.

The French had entered Kelung harbor and the danger was growing more serious every day when Mackay found it necessary to go to Palm Island, a pretty islet in the mouth of the Kelung river. It was almost courting death to go, but he had been sent for, and he went. He found the place right under the French guns and in the midst of raging Chinese. Some of the faithful students were there, and they were overcome with joy and hope at the sight of him. He gathered them about him in a mission house for prayer and a word of encouragement. Outside the Chinese soldiers paraded up and down. Sometimes indeed they would burst into the room and threaten the inmates with violence should the French fire. Kai Bok-su went on quietly talking to his students. He urged them to be faithful and reminded them of what their Master suffered at the hands of a mob for their sake. But, in spite of their brave spirits, the little company could not help listening for the boom of the French guns. It was fully expected that the enemy would soon fire, and when they did, the Christians well knew there would be little chance for them to escape.

But God had prepared a way out of the difficulty. The meeting was scarcely over when a messenger came in, asking for the missionary. A Christian on the mainland was very ill and wanted Kai Bok-su to visit him. Mackay with his students left the island at once and went to the home of the sick man.

They had been gone but a short time when the thunder of the French cannon broke over the harbor. The guns from the Chinese fort answered, and had the missionary been on Palm Island he and his converts would surely have been killed.

The Chinese were no match for the French gunners. The bombardment destroyed the fort and killed every soldier who did not manage to get away. A great shell crashed into the magazine of the fort, and the explosion hurled masses of the concrete walls an incredible distance. The city about the fort was completely deserted, for the people fled at the first sound of the guns.

As soon as the firing was over, the rabble broke loose and a perfect reign of terror prevailed. The mob carried black flags and swept over town and country, plundering and murdering. The Christians were of course the first object of attack, and to tear down a church was the mob's fiercest joy. Seven of the most beautiful chapels were completely destroyed and many others injured.

In the town of Toa-liong-pong was the home of Koa Kau, one of Kai Bok-su's most devoted students. Here was a lovely chapel built at great expense. The crowd tore it to pieces from roof to foundation. Then, out of the bricks of the ruin they erected a huge pile, eight feet high; they plastered it over with mud, and on the face of it, next the highway where every one might see it, they wrote in large Chinese characters:

MACKAY, THE BLACK-BEARDED BARBARIAN, LIES HERE. HIS WORK IS ENDED.

They knew that the first was not true, but they firmly believed the latter statement, for they understood little of the power of the gospel.

At Sin-tiam the crowd of ruffians smashed the doors and windows of the church. Then they took the communion roll and read aloud the names of the Christians who had been baptized. As each name was announced, some of the murderers would rush off toward the home of the one mentioned. Here they would torture and often kill the members of the family. The native preacher and his family barely escaped with their lives. One good old Christian man with his wife, both over sixty, were dragged out into the deep water of the Sin-tiam river. Here they were given a choice. If they gave up Jesus Christ, their lives would be saved. If they still remained Christians, they would be drowned right there and then. The brave old couple refused to accept life at such a cost.

"I'm not ashamed to own my Lord," was a hymn Kai Bok-su had taught them, and they had meant every word as they had sung it many times in the pretty chapel by the river. And so they were "not ashamed" now. They were led deeper and deeper into the water, and at every few feet the way of escape was offered, but they steadily refused, and were at last flung into the river—faithful martyrs who certainly won a crown of life.

These were only two among many brave Christians who died for their Master's sake. Some were put to tortures too horrible to tell to make them give up their faith. Some were hung by their hair to trees, some were kicked or beaten to death, many were slashed with knives until death relieved their pain. And on every side the most noble Christian heroism was shown. In all ages there have been those who died for their faith in Jesus Christ; and these Formosan followers of their Master proved themselves no less faithful than the martyrs of old.

And where was Kai Bok-su while the mob raged over the country? Going about his work in Tamsui as of old. Only now he worked both night and day, and the anxiety for his poor converts kept him awake in the few hours when he might have snatched some sleep. He was here, there, everywhere at once, it seemed, writing letters to encourage the Christians in distress, visiting those who were wavering to strengthen their faith, teaching his students, praying, preaching, night and day, he never ceased; and always the mob surged about him threatening his life.

The French ships now sailed out of Kelung harbor and took up their position opposite Tamsui. Every one knew this probably meant bombardment, and Dr. Mackay and Mr. Jamieson, standing on the bluff before their houses, looked at each other and each knew the other's thought. Bombardment would mean that the mob would come raging up and destroy both life and property on the hill.

But just as they expected the roar of guns to open, there sailed into Tamsui harbor a vessel that flew a different flag from the French. Mackay, looking at her through a glass, made out with joy the crosses on the red banner of Britain! England had nothing to do with this Chinese-French war, but as a British vessel can be found lying around almost any port in the wide world, there of course happened to be one near Tamsui. She gained a passport into the harbor and sailed in with a very kindly mission; it was to protect the lives of foreigners, not only from the French guns, but from the Chinese mobs.

The ship had been in the harbor but a short time when a young English naval officer, carrying the British flag, came up the path to the houses on the bluff. Dr. Mackay was in the library of Oxford College, lecturing to his students, when the visitor entered.

The missionary made the sailor welcome and the young man told his errand. Dr. Mackay was invited to bring his family and his valuables and come on board the vessel to be the guest of the captain until the disturbance was over.

It was a most kindly invitation and Dr. Mackay shook his visitor's hand warmly as he thanked him. He turned and translated the message to his students, and their hearts stood still with dismay. If Kai Bok-su, their stay and support, were to be taken away, what would become of them? But Kai Bok-su had not changed with the changing circumstances. He was still as brave and undaunted as though trouble had never come to his island.

He turned to the officer again with a smile. "My family would not be hard to move," he said, "but my valuables—I am afraid I could not take them." He made a gesture toward the students standing about him. "These young men and many more converts scattered all over north Formosa, are my valuables. Many of them have faced death unflinchingly for my sake. They are my valuables, and I cannot leave them."

It was bravely said, just as Kai Bok-su might be expected to speak, and the English officer's eyes kindled with appreciation. The words found a ready response in his heart. They were the words of a true soldier of the King. The officer went back to his captain with Mackay's message and with a deep admiration in his heart for the man who would rather face death than leave his friends.

So the British man-of-war drew off, leaving the missionaries in the midst of danger. And almost immediately, with a great bursting roar, the bombardment from the French ships opened. Sometimes the shells flew high over the town and up to the bluff, so Dr. and Mrs. Mackay put their three little ones in a safe corner under the house; but they themselves as well as Mr. and Mrs. Jamieson, went in and out to and from the college, and the girls' school as though nothing were happening.

Every day Mackay's work grew heavier and his anxiety for the persecuted Christians grew deeper. He ate very little, and he scarcely slept at all. It was not the noise of the carnage about him that kept him awake. He would have fallen asleep peacefully amidst bursting shells, but he had no opportunity. The whole burden of the young Church, harassed by persecution on all sides, seemed to rest upon his spirit. Anxiety for the Christians in the inland stations from whom he could not hear weighed on him night and day, and his brave spirit was put to the severest test.

Only his great strong faith in God kept him up and kept up the spirits of the converts who looked to him for an example. And a brave pattern he showed them. Often he and A Hoa paced the lawn in front of the house while shot and shell whizzed around them. During the worst of the bombardment they came and went between the college and the house as if they had charmed lives. One day there was a great roar and a shell struck Oxford College, shaking it to its foundations. The smoke from fort and ships had scarcely cleared away when, crash! and the girls' school was struck by a bursting shell. Next moment there was a fearful bang and a great stone that stood in front of the Mackays' house went up into the air in a thousand fragments.

But when the firing was hottest, Kai Bok-su would repeat to his students the comforting Psalm:

"Thou shalt not be afraid for the terror by night; nor for the arrow that flieth by day."

But in spite of his brave demeanor, the strain on the shepherd of this harassed flock was beginning to tell. And when the bombardment ceased and the intense anxiety for his loved ones was over, Kai Bok-su suddenly collapsed. Dr. Johnsen, the foreign physician of Tamsui, came hurriedly up to the mission house to see him. His verdict sent a thrill of dismay through every heart that loved him, from the anxious little wife by the patient's side, to the poorest convert in the town below. Their beloved Kai Bok-su had brain fever.

"Too much anxiety and too little sleep,"

said the medical man. "He must sleep now," he added, "or he will die." But now that Kai Bok-su had a chance to rest, he could not. Sleep had been chased away too long to stay with him. Night and day he tossed about, wide awake and burning with fever. His temperature was never less than 102 during those days, and all the doctor's efforts could not lower it. The awful heat of September was on, and the great typhoons that would soon sweep across the country and clear the air had not yet come. The glaring sun and the stifling damp heat were all against the patient. At last one day the doctor saw a crisis was approaching. He stood looking down at the hot, flushed face, at the burning eyes, and the restless hands that were never still, and he said to himself, "If the fever does not go down to-day, he will die."

The doctor went along "College Road" toward his home, answering the eager, anxious questions that met him on all sides with only a shake of his head.

A Hoa followed him, his drawn face full

of pleading. Was he no better? he asked with quivering lips. It was the question poor A Hoa asked many, many times a day, for he never left the house when not away on duty. The doctor's face was full of sympathy and his own heart weighed down as he sadly answered, "No."

"If I only had some ice," he muttered, knowing well he had none. "If there was only one bit of ice in Tamsui, I'd save him yet."

Over in the British consulate Dr. Johnsen had another patient. Mr. Dodd lay sick there, though not nearly as ill as the missionary, and the physician's next visit was to him. When he entered he found a servant carrying a tray with some ice on it to the sick room.

"Ice!" cried the doctor, overjoyed. "Where did it come from?"

The servant explained that the steamship *Hailoong* had just arrived in Tamsui harbor with it that morning. The doctor entered Mr. Dodd's room. Would he give him that ice to save Mackay's life? was the question he asked. To save such a life as Mackay's! That was an absurd question, Mr. Dodd declared, and he immediately ordered that every bit of ice he had should be sent at once to the missionary's house.

The doctor hurried back up the hill with the precious remedy. He broke up a piece and laid it like a little cushion on poor Kai Bok-su's hot forehead; that forehead beneath which the busy brain, resting neither day nor night, was burning up. It had not been there a great while before the restless eyes lost their fire, the eyelids drooped and, wonderful sight, Kai Bok-su sank into a sleep! The doctor hardly dared to breathe If he could only be kept asleep now, he had a chance. Dr. Mackay had never been a sleeper, he well knew. He was too restless, too energetic, to allow himself even proper rest. When Dr. Fraser, his first assistant, had been with him, he had struggled to persuade him to stay in bed at least six hours every night, but not always with success. But now he was to show what he could do in the matter of sleeping. All that night he lay, breathing peacefully, the next day he slept on from morning till night, and little by little the ice melted away on his forehead. He did not move all the next night, and A Hoa and Mrs. Mackay and the doctor took turns at his bedside watching that the precious ice was always there. Morning came and it was all finished. The patient opened his eyes. He had slept thirty-six hours, and a thrill of joy went through every Christian heart in Tamsui, for their Kai Bok-su was saved!

But though the crisis was over, he was still very weak, and such was the state of affairs through the country that he was in no condition to cope with them. Riot and plunder was the order of the day. News of churches being destroyed, of faithful Christians being tortured or put to death, were still coming to the mission house, and no one could tell what day would bring Kai Bok-su's turn.

And now came an order from the British consul which the missionaries could not disobey. He commanded that their families must be moved at once from Formosa, as he could not answer for their protection. So at once preparations for their departure were made, and Mr. Jamieson took his wife and Mrs. Mackay and her three little ones and sailed away for Hongkong.

But once more Kai Bok-su stayed behind. It cost him bitter pain to part with his loved ones, knowing he might never see them again; he was weak and spent with fever, and his poor body was worn to a shadow, but he stubbornly refused to leave the men who had stood by him in every danger. The consul commanded, the doctor pleaded, but no, Kai Bok-su would not go. If the danger had grown greater, then all the more reason why he should stay and comfort his people. And if God were pleased to send death, then they would all die together.

But he was so weak and sick that the doctor feared that if he remained there would be little chance for the mob to kill him: death would come sooner. So he came to his stubborn patient with a new proposition. The *Fukien,* a merchant steamship, was now lying in Tamsui harbor. She was to run to Hongkong and back directly. If Mackay would only take that trip, his physician urged, the sea air would make him new again, and he would return in a short time and be ready to take up his work once more.

It was that promise that moved Mackay's resolution. His utter weakness held him down from work, and he longed with all his soul to go out through the country to help the poor, suffering churches. So he finally consented to take the short journey and pay a visit to his dear ones in Hongkong.

He did not get back quite as soon as he intended, for the French blockade delayed his vessel. But at last he stepped out upon the Tamsui dock into a crowd of preachers, students, and converts who were weeping for joy about him and exclaiming over his improved looks.

The voyage had certainly done wonders for him, and at once he declared he must take a trip into the country and visit those who were left of the churches.

It was a desperate undertaking, for

French soldiers were now scattered through the country, guarding the larger towns and cities and everywhere mobs of furious Chinese were ready to torture or kill every foreigner. But it would take even greater difficulties than these to stop Kai Bok-su, and he began at once to lay plans for going on a tour.

He first went to the British consul and came back in high spirits with a folded paper in his hand. He spread it out on the library table before A Hoa and Sun-a, who were to go with him, and this is what it said:

British Consulate, Tamsui,
May 27th, 1885.

To the Officer in Chief Command of the French Forces at Kelung:

The bearer of this paper, the Rev. George Leslie Mackay, D.D., a British subject, missionary in Formosa, wishes to enter Kelung, to visit his chapel and his house there, and to proceed through Kelung to Kap-tsu-lan on the east coast of Formosa to visit his converts there. Wherefore I, the undersigned, consul for Great Britain at Tamsui, do beg the officer in chief command of the French forces in Kelung to grant the said George Leslie Mackay entry into, and a free and safe passage through, Kelung. He will be accompanied by two Chinese followers, belonging to his mission, named, respectively, Giam Chheng Hoa, and Iap Sun.

A. Frater,
Her Britannic Majesty's Consul at Tamsui.

They had all the power of the British Empire behind them so long as they held that paper. Then they hired a burden-bearer to carry their food, and Mackay cut a bamboo pole, fully twenty feet long, and on it tied the British flag. With this floating over them, the little army marched through the rice-fields down to Kelung.

It was an adventurous journey. But, wonderful though it seemed, they came through it safely. Poor Kai Bok-su's heart was torn as he saw the ravages the mob had made on his churches. But what a cheer his heart received when he found that persecution had strengthened the converts that were left and everywhere the heathen marveled that men should die for the faith the barbarian missionary had taught.

They were taken prisoners once for German spies, and led far out of their way. But they came back to Tamsui safely, having greatly cheered the faithful Christians who still were true to their Master, Jesus Christ. It was early in June, just one year from the opening of the war, that the French sailed away. They were disgusted with the whole affair, the commander of one vessel told Dr. Mackay, and they were all very glad it was over.

Mr. and Mrs. Jamieson and Dr. Mackay's family returned to their homes on the bluff, and work started up again with its old vigor.

But everywhere the heathen were in great glee. Christianity had been destroyed with the chapels, they were sure. Wherever Mackay went, shouts of derision followed him, and everywhere he could hear the joyful cry "Long-tsong bo-khi!" which meant "The mission is wiped out!"

But strange though it may seem, the mission had never been stronger, and it soon began to assert itself. Dr. Mackay went at the work of repairing the lost buildings with all the force of his nature. First, he and

Mr. Jamieson and A Hoa sat down and prepared a statement of their losses. This they sent to the commander-in-chief of the Chinese forces, who had been responsible for law and order. Without any delay or questioning of the missionaries' rights, the general sent Dr. Mackay the sum asked for—ten thousand Mexican dollars.[1]

The next thing was to plan the new chapels and see to the building of them. And before the shouts of "Long-tsong bo-khi" had well started, they began to be contradicted by walls of brick or stone that rose up strong and sure to show that the mission had not been wiped out. Three of the chapels were commenced all at once—at Sin-tiam, at Bang-kah and at Sek-khau. Before anything was done Dr. Mackay and a party of his students went up to Sin-tiam to look over the site. They stood up on the pile of ruins, surrounded by the Christians, and a crowd of heathen came around gleefully to watch them in the hopes of seeing their despair.

[1] About $5,000.

But to their amazement the little company of Christians led by the wonderful Kai Bok-su, suddenly burst into a hymn of praise to God who had brought them safely through all their troubles:

Bless, O my soul, the Lord thy God,
  And not forgetful be
Of all his gracious benefits
  He hath bestowed on thee!

The heathen listened in wonder to the words of praise where they had expected lamentation, and they asked each other what was this strange power that made men so strong and brave.

And their amazement grew as the chapels, the lovely new chapels of stone or brick, began to rise from the ruins of the old ones. And not only did the old ones reappear, new and more beautiful, but as Dr. Mackay and his native preachers went here and there over the country others peeped forth like the hepaticas of springtime, until there were not only the forty original chapels, but in a few years the number had increased to sixty.

The triumphant shout that the mission had been wiped out ceased completely, and the people declared that they had been fools to try to destroy the chapels, for the result had been only bigger and better ones.

"Look now," said one old heathen, pointing a withered finger to the handsome spire of the Bang-kah chapel, that lifted itself toward the sky, "Look now, the chapel towers above our temple. It is larger than the one we destroyed."

His neighbors crowding about him and gazing up with superstitious awe at the spire, agreed.

"If we touch this one he will build another and a bigger one," remarked another man.

"We cannot stop the barbarian missionary," said the old heathen with an air of conviction.

"No, no one can stop the great Kai Boksu," they finally agreed, and so they left off all opposition in despair.

Yes, the cry of "Long-tsong bo-khi" had died, and the answer to it was inscribed on the front of the splendid chapels that sprang up all over north Formosa. For, just above the main entrance to each, worked out in stucco plaster, was a picture of the burning bush, and around it in Chinese the grand old motto:

"Nec tamen consumebatur" ("Yet it was not consumed.")

TRIUMPHAL MARCH

CHAPTER XII

TRIUMPHAL MARCH

UP and down the length and breadth of north Formosa, seeming to be in two or three places at once, went Kai Bok-su, during this time of reviving after the war. He would be in Kelung to-day superintending the new chapel building, in Tamsui at Oxford College the next day, in Bang-kah preaching a short while after, and no one could tell just where the next day.

But every one did know that wherever he went, Christians grew stronger and heathen gave up their idols.

The Kap-tsu-lan plain, away on the eastern coast, seemed to be a sort of pet among all his mission fields, and he was always turning his steps thither. For the Pe-po-hoan who lived there, while they were simple and warm-hearted and easily moved by the gospel story, were not such strong characters as the Chinese. So the missionary felt he must visit them often to help steady their faith.

Not long after the close of the war, he set off on a trip to the Kap-tsu-lan plain. Besides his students, he was accompanied by a young German scientist. Dr. Warburg had come from Germany to Formosa to collect peculiar plants and flowers and to find any old weapons or relics of interest belonging to the savage tribes. All these were for the use of the university in Germany which had sent him out.

The young scientist was delighted with Dr. Mackay and found in him a very interesting companion. They met in Kelung, and when Dr. Warburg found that Dr. Mackay was going to visit the Kap-tsu-lan plain, he joined his party. The stranger found many rare specimens of orchids on that trip and several peculiar spear and arrow heads to be taken back as curios to Germany. But he found something rarer and more wonderful and something for which he had not come to search.

He saw in one place three hundred people gather about their missionary and raise a ringing hymn of praise to the God of heaven, of whom they had not so much as heard but a few short years before. He visited sixteen little chapels and heard clever, bright-faced young Chinese preachers stand up in them and tell the old, old story of Jesus and his love. And he realized that these things were far more wonderful than the rarest curios he could find in all Formosa.

When he bade good-by to Dr. Mackay, he said: "I never saw anything like this before. If scientific skeptics had traveled with a missionary as I have and witnessed what I have witnessed on this plain, they would assume a different attitude toward the heralds of the cross."

Not many months later Dr. Mackay again went down the eastern coast. This time he took three of his closest friends, all preacher students, Tan He, Sun-a, and Koa Kau. With a coolie to carry provisions, their Bibles, their forceps, and some malaria medicine, they started off fully equipped.

By steam launch to Bang-kah, by a queer little railway train to Tsui-tng-kha and by foot to Kelung was the first part of the journey. The next part was a tramp over the mountains to Kap-tsu-lan.

The road now grew rough and dangerous. Overhead hung loose rocks, huge enough to crush the whole party should they fall. Underneath were wet, slippery stones which might easily make one go sliding down into the chasm below.

As usual on this trip they had many hair-breadth escapes, for there were savages too hiding up in the dense forest and waiting an opportunity to spring out upon the travelers. Dr. Mackay was almost caught in a small avalanche also. He leaped over a narrow stream-bed, and as he did so, he dislodged a loose mass of rock above him. It came down with a fearful crash, scattering the smaller pieces right upon his heels; but they passed all dangers safely and toward evening reached the shore where the great long Pacific billows rolled upon the sand. They were in the Kap-tsu-lan plain.

Their journey through the plain was like a triumphal march. Wherever a chapel had been erected, there were converts to be examined; wherever there was no chapel, the people gathered about the missionary and pleaded for one. They often recalled the first visit of Kai Bok-su when "No room for barbarians" were the only words that met him.

But Dr. Mackay wished to go farther on this journey than he had ever gone. Some distance south of Kap-tsu-lan lay another district called the Ki-lai plain. The people here were also aborigines of the island who had been conquered by the Chinese like the Pepo-hoan. But the inhabitants of Ki-lai were called Lam-si-hoan, which means "Barbarians of the south." Dr. Mackay had never been among them, but they had heard the gospel. A missionary from Oxford College had journeyed away down there to tell the people about Jesus and had been working among them for some years. He was not a graduate, not even a student—but only the cook! For Oxford College was such a place of inspiration under Kai Bok-su, that even the servants in the kitchen wanted to go out and preach the gospel. So the cook had gone away to the Ki-lai plain, and, ever since he had left, Dr. Mackay had longed to go and see how his work was prospering.

So at one of the most southerly points of the Kap-tsu-lan plain he secured a boat for the voyage south. The best he could get was a small craft quite open, only twelve feet long. It was not a very fine vessel with which to brave the Pacific Ocean, but where was the crazy craft in which Kai Bok-su would not embark to go and tell the gospel to the heathen? The boat was manned by six Pe-po-hoan rowers, all Christians, and at five o'clock in the evening they pushed out into the surf of So Bay. A crowd of converts came down to the shore to bid them farewell. As the boat shoved off the friends on the beach started a hymn. The rowers and the missionaries caught it up and the two groups joined, the sound of each growing fainter and fainter to the other as the distance widened.

All lands to God in joyful sounds
  Aloft your voices raise,
Sing forth the honor of his name,
  And glorious make his praise!

And the land and the sea, answering each other, joined in praise to him who was the Maker of both.

And so the rowers pulled away in time to the swing of the Psalm, the boat rounded a point, and the beloved figure of Kai Bok-su disappeared from sight.

Away down the coast the oarsmen pulled, and the four missionaries squeezed themselves into as small a space as possible to be out of the way of the oars. All the evening they rowed steadily, and as they still swept along night came down suddenly. They kept close to the shore, where to their right arose great mountains straight up from the water's edge. They were covered with forest, and here and there in the blackness fires twinkled.

"Head-hunters!" said the helmsman, pointing toward them.

Away to the left stretched the Pacific

Ocean, and above shone the stars in the deep blue dome. It was a still, hot tropical night. From the land came the heavy scent of flowers. The only sound that broke the stillness was the regular thud, thud of the oars or the cry of some wild animal floating out from the jungle. As they passed on through the warm darkness, the sea took on that wonderful fiery glow that so often burns on the oceans of the tropics. Every wave became a blaze of phosphorescence. Every ripple from the oars ran away in many-colored flames—red, green, blue, and orange. Kai Bok-su, sitting amazed at the glory to which the Pe-po-hoan boatmen had become accustomed, was silent with awe. He had seen the phosphorescent lights often before, but never anything like this. He put his hand down into the molten sea and scooped up handfuls of what seemed drops of liquid fire. And as his fingers dipped into the water they shone like rods of red-hot iron. Over the gleaming iridescent surface, sparks of fire darted like lightning, and from the little boat's sides flashed out flames of gold and rose and amber. It was grand. And no wonder they all joined—Chinese, Malayan, and Canadian—in making the dark cliffs and the gleaming sea echo to the strains of praise to the One who had created all this glory.

O come let us sing to the Lord,
  To him our voices raise
With joyful noise, let us the rock
  Of our salvation praise.

To him the spacious sea belongs,
  For he the same did make;
The dry land also from his hand
  Its form at first did take.

Dawn came up out of the Pacific with a new glory of light and color that dispelled the wonders of the night. It showed the voyagers that they were very near a low shore where it would be possible to land. But the helmsman shook his head at the proposal. He pointed out huts along the line of forest and figures on the shore. And then with a common impulse, the rowers swung round and pulled straight out to sea; for with Pe-po-hoan experience they saw at once that here was a savage village, and not long would their heads remain on their shoulders should they touch land.

The scorching sun soon poured its hot rays upon the tired rowers, but they pulled steadily. They too, like Kai Bok-su, were anxious to take this great good news of Jesus Christ to those who had not yet learned of him. When safely out of reach of the head-hunters, they once more turned south, and, about noon, tired and hot, at last approached the first port of the Ki-lai plain. Every one drew a sigh of relief, for the men had been rowing steadily all night and half the day. As they drew near Dr. Mackay looked eagerly at the queer village. It appeared to be half Chinese and half Lam-si-hoan. It consisted of two rows of small thatched houses with a street between nearly two hundred feet wide.

The rowers ran the boat up on the sloping pebbly beach and all stepped out with much relief to stretch their stiffened limbs. They had scarcely done so when a military officer came down the shore and approaching Dr. Mackay made him welcome with the greatest warmth. There was a military encampment here, and this was the officer as well as the headman of the village. He invited Dr. Mackay and his friends to take dinner with him. Dr. Mackay accepted with pleased surprise. This was far better than he had expected. He was still more surprised to hear his name on every hand.

"It is the great Kai Bok-su," could be heard in tones of deepest respect from fishermen at their nets and old women by the door and children playing with their kites in the wide street.

"How do they know me?" he asked, as he was greeted by a rice-seller, sitting at the open front of his shop.

"Ah, we have heard of you and your work in the north, Pastor Mackay," said his host, smiling, "and our people want to hear of this new Jehovah-religion too.

The cook-missionary had evidently spread wonderful reports of Kai Bok-su and his gospel and so prepared the way. He was preaching just then in a place called Ka-le-oan, farther inland. When the officer learned that Dr. Mackay wanted to visit him he turned to his servant with a most surprising order. It was to saddle his pony and bring him for Kai Bok-su to ride to Ka-le-oan.

The pony came, sleek and plump and with a string of jingling bells adorning him. A pony was a wonderful sight in Formosa, and Dr. Mackay had not used any sort of animal in his work since that disastrous day when he had tried in vain to ride the stubborn Lu-a. But now he gladly mounted the sedate little steed and trotted away along the narrow pathway between the rice-fields toward Ka-le-oan.

Darkness had almost descended when he rode into the village and stopped before a small grass-covered bamboo dwelling where the cook-preacher lived. For years the people here had looked for Kai Bok-su's coming, for years they had talked of this great event, and for years their preacher had been writing and saying as he received his reply from the eager missionary in Tamsui, "He may come soon."

And now he was really here! The sound of his horse's bells had scarcely stopped before the preacher's house, when the news began to spread like fire through the village. The preacher, who had worked so hard and waited so long, wept for joy, and before he could make Dr. Mackay welcome in a proper manner the room was filled with men, all wildly eager for a sight of the great Kai Bok-su, while outside a crowd gathered about the door striving to get even a glimpse of him. The ex-cook of Oxford College had preached so faithfully that many were already converted to Christianity, many more knew a good deal of the gospel, and crowds were ready to throw away their idols. They were weary of their heathen rites and superstitions. They were longing for something better, they scarcely knew what.

"But the mandarin will not let them become Christians," said the preacher anxiously. "It is he who is keeping them from decision. He has said that they must continue in idolatry, as a token of loyalty to China."

"Are you sure that is true?" cried Dr. Mackay.

The converts nodded. They had "heard" it said at least.

But Kai Bok-su was not the man to accept mere hearsay. He was always wisely careful to avoid any collision with the authorities. But remembering the kindness shown him back in Hoe-lien-kang, he could not quite believe that the mandarin who had been so kind to him could be hostile to the religion of Jesus Christ.

To think was to act, and early the next morning, he was riding back to the seacoast, to inquire how much of this rumor was true.

His reception was very warm. It was all right, the officer declared. Whatever had been said or done in the past must be forgotten. Kai Bok-su might go where he pleased and preach his Jehovah-religion to whomsoever he would.

It was a very light-hearted rider the pony carried as he galloped back along the narrow paths, with the good news for the villagers. The word went round as soon as he arrived. Kai Bok-su wanted to know how many were for the true God. All who would worship him were at once to clear their houses of idols and declare that they would serve Jehovah and him only. At dark a great crowd gathered in an open space in the village. Representatives from five villages were there, chiefs were shouting to their people, and when Dr. Mackay and his students arrived, the place was all noise and confusion. He was puzzled. It almost looked as if there was to be a riot, though the voices did not sound angry.

He climbed up on a pile of rubbish and his face shone clear in the light of the flaring torches. His voice rang out loud and commanding above the tumult.

"What is this noise about?" he cried. "Is there a difference of opinion among you as to whether you shall worship these poor toys of wood and stone, or the true God who is your Father?"

He paused and as if from one man came back the answer in a mighty shout:

"No, we will worship the true God!"

The tumult had been one of enthusiasm and not of dispute!

Kai Bok-su's heart gave a great bound. For a moment he could not speak. He who had so often stood up fearless and bold before a raging heathen mob, now faltered before this sea of eager faces, upturned to him. It seemed too good to be true that all this crowd, representing five villages, was anxious to become followers of the God of heaven. His voice grew steady at last, and standing up there in the flickering torchlight he told those children of the plain what it meant to be a follower of Jesus Christ. It was a late hour when the meeting broke up, but even then Dr. Mackay could not go to bed. Never since the day that A Hoa, his first convert, had accepted Jesus Christ as his Savior, had he felt such joy, and all night he walked up and down in front of the preacher's house, unable to sleep for the thankfulness to God that surged in his heart.

Morning brought a wonderful day for the

Ki-lai plain. It was like a day when freedom from slavery was announced. Had there been bells in the village they would certainly have been rung. But joy bells were ringing in every heart. Nobody could work all day. The rice-fields and the shops and the pottery works lay idle. There was but one business to do that day, and that was to get rid of their idols.

Early in the morning the mayor of the place, or the headman as he was called, came to the house to invite the missionary and his party to join him. Behind him walked four big boys, carrying two large wicker baskets, hanging from poles across their shoulders; and behind them came the whole village, men, women, and children, their faces shining with a new joy. The procession moved along from house to house. At every place it stopped and out from the home were carried idols, ancestral tablets, mock-money, flags, incense sticks, and all the stuff used in idol worship. These were all emptied into the baskets carried by the boys. When even the temple had been ransacked and the work of clearing out the idols in the village was finished, the procession moved on to the next hamlet. The villages were very near each other, so the journey was not wearisome; and at last when every vestige of the old idolatrous life had been taken from the homes of five villages, the happy crowd marched back to the first village. There was a large courtyard near the temple and here the procession halted. The boys dropped their well-filled baskets, and their contents were piled in the center of the court. The people gathered about the heap and with shouts of joy set fire to these signs of their lifelong slavery. Soon the pile was blazing and crackling, and all the people, even the chiefs of the villages, vied with each other in burning up the idols they had so lately besought for blessings.

And then they turned toward the heathen temple and delivered it over to Kai Bok-su for a chapel in which he and his students might preach the gospel.

And so the temple was lighted up for a new kind of worship. It had been used for worship many, many times before, but oh, how different it was this time! Instead of coming in fear of demons, dread of their gods' anger, and determination to cheat them if possible, these poor folk crowded into the new-old temple with light, happy hearts, as children coming to their Father. And was not God their Father, only they had not known him before?

The heathen temple was dedicated to the worship of the true God by singing the old but always new, one hundredth Psalm. The Lam-si-hoan were not very good singers. They had not much idea of tune. They had less idea of just when to start, and there was very little to be said about the harmony of those hundreds of voices. But in spite of it all, Kai Bok-su had to confess that never in the music of his homeland or in the more finished harmonies of Europe, had he heard anything so grandly uplifting as when those newly-freed people stood up in their idol temple and with heart and soul and voice unitedly poured forth in thunderous volume of praise the great command:

All people that on earth do dwell,
Sing to the Lord with cheerful voice.

For a whole week with his pony and groom, which were still his to do with as he pleased, the busy missionary rode up and down this plain, visiting the villages, preaching, and teaching the people how to live as Jesus Christ their Savior had lived; for it was necessary to impress upon their childlike minds that it would be of no use to burn up the idols in their homes and temple unless they also gave up the still more harmful idols in their hearts.

But at last the day came when the pony had to be returned to its owner and the missionary and his helpers must leave. It was a sad day but a joyous one—the day that great visit came to an end. Crowds of Christians, fain to keep him, followed him down to the shore, and many kindly but reluctant hands shoved the little boat out into the surf. And as the rowers sent it skimming out over the great Pacific rollers, there rose from the beach the parting hymn, the one that had dedicated the heathen temple to the worship of the true God:

> All people that on earth do dwell,
> Sing to the Lord with cheerful voice.

and from the rowers and the missionaries in the boat, came back the glad echo:

> Know that the Lord is God indeed
> Without our aid he did us make.

They were soon out of sight. The rowers pulled hard, but a stiff northeaster straight from Japan was blowing against them, and they made but little headway. Night came down, and they were again skirting those dark cliffs, where, here and there, along the narrow strip of sand, the night-fires of the savages flamed out against the dark tangle of foliage. All night long the rowers struggled against the wind. They were afraid to go out far for the waves were wild, they dared not land, for, crueler than the sea, the head-hunters waited for them on the shore. And so all that night, taking turns with the rowers, the missionary and his students toiled against the wind and wave. The dawn came up gray and stormy, and they were still tossing about among the white billows. No one had touched food for twenty-four hours. They had rice in the boat, but there was no place where they dared land to have it cooked. There was nothing to do but to pull, pull at the oars, and a weary task it seemed, for the boat appeared to make little headway, and the rowers barely succeeded in keeping her from being dashed upon the rocks.

They were becoming almost too weak to keep any control over their boat, when about three o'clock in the afternoon they managed to round a point. There before them curved a beautiful bay. Behind it and on both sides arose a perpendicular wall several hundred feet high. At its foot stretched a narrow sandy beach. It was an ideal spot, secure from savages both by land and sea. A shout of encouragement from Kai Bok-su was the one thing needed. Tired arms and aching backs bent to the oars for one last effort, and when the boat swept up on the sandy beach every one uttered a heartfelt prayer of thankfulness to the Father who had provided this little haven in a time of such distress.

The rest of the journey was made safely, and just forty days after their departure the four missionaries returned, worn out, to Tamsui.

THE LAND OCCUPIED

CHAPTER XIII

THE LAND OCCUPIED

BUT Kai Bok-su had no sooner returned than he was off again. He was not one of that sort who could settle down after an achievement, content to rest for a little. He seemed to forget all about what had been done and was "up and at it again." If he "did not know when he was beaten," neither did he seem to know when he was successful; and like Alexander the Great he was always sighing for new worlds to conquer, yes, and marching off and conquering them too.

But every time he returned to his work at Tamsui from one of these tours, it was borne in upon him more forcibly every day that his faithful assistant who was left in charge, could not long shoulder his work. Mr. Jamieson was fighting a losing battle with ill health. The terrible experiences during the war year, the hard work, and the trying Formosan climate had all combined against him. His brave spirit could not always sustain the body that was growing gradually weaker, and one day, a dark, sad day, the devoted soul was set free from the poor pain-racked body. He had given eight years of hard, faithful work to the study of the language and to the service of the Master in the mission. Mrs. Jamieson returned to Canada, and once more Dr. Mackay faced the work, unaided except by native preachers. But he was not daunted even by this bereavement, for he always lived in the perfect faith that God was on his side.

And then, he had by this time three new assistants in the mission-house on the bluff. They did not even guess that they were any help to him, for they could never go with him on his mission tours. But by their sweet merry ways and their joyous welcome to father, when he returned, they did help him greatly, and made his home-comings a delight.

"How many did you baptize, father?"

was baby George's inevitable question on his father's return. For already the wise toddler had learned something of the bitter enmity of the heathen world, and knew that converts meant friends. Then father's home-coming meant presents too, wonderful things, bows and arrows, rare curios for the museum in the college, and, once, a pair of the funniest monkeys in the world, which proved most entertaining playthings for the little boy and his two sisters. Another time the father brought home a young bear to keep the monkeys company, but they were not at all polite to their guest, for they made poor bruin's life miserable by teasing him. They would torment him until he would stamp with rage. But he was not always badly used, for when the three children would come out to feed him, he was very happy, and he would show his pleasure by putting his head between his paws and rolling over and over like a big ball of fur. And he always seemed quite proud of his performance when his three little keepers shrieked with laughter.

The next year after Mr. Jamieson's death the empty mission-house was once more filled. In September the Rev. Mr. William and Mrs. Gauld sailed from Canada, and with their arrival Dr. Mackay took new heart.

The new missionaries had learned the language and their work was well under way when the time came round once more for Dr. Mackay to go back to Canada for a year's rest. This time there was quite a little party went with him: his wife, their three children, and Koa Kau, one of his students.

Among those left to assist Mr. Gauld, there was none he relied upon more than A Hoa. Mr. Gauld, at the close of his second year's work, wrote of this fellow worker: "The longer and better I know him, the more I can love him, trust his honesty, and respect his judgment. He knows his own people, from the governor of the island to the ragged opium-smoking beggar, and has influence with them all."

There were many others besides A Hoa to

Dr. G. L. Mackay, Wife, and Three Children

render the missionary faithful help; among them Sun-a and Tan He, the latter pastor of the church of Sin-tiam; and just because Kai Bok-su was away they worked the harder, that he might receive a good report of them on his return.

The separation was longer this time, for Dr. Mackay wished to send his children to school, and he decided that they would remain in Canada two years. He was made Moderator of the General Assembly, too, and the Church at home needed him to stir them up to a greater desire to help those beyond the seas.

While he was working and preaching in Canada, his heart turned always to his beloved Formosa, and letters from the friends there were among his greatest pleasures. A Hoa's, of course, were doubly welcome. Pastor Giam, the name by which he was now called, was Mr. Gauld's right-hand helper in those days, and once he went alone on a tour away to the eastern shore. While there he had an adventure of which he wrote to Kai Bok-su.

"The other morning while walking on the seashore I saw a sailing-vessel slowly drifting shoreward and in danger of being wrecked, for there was a fog and a heavy sea. I hastened back to the chapel and beat the drum to call the villagers to worship. As soon as it was over I asked converts and heathen to go in their fishing-boats as quickly as possible and let the sailors know they need not fear savages there, and if they wished to come ashore a chapel would be given them to stay in. The whole crew came ashore in the boats at once. I gave your old room to the captain, his wife and child, and other accommodation to the rest. I then hurried away to a mandarin and asked him to send men to protect the ship."

When Kai Bok-su read the story and remembered that, twenty-five years earlier, the crew of that vessel would have been murdered and their ship plundered, he exclaimed with joy, "Blessed Christianity! Surely,

Blessings abound where'er He reigns!"

A Hoa had another tale to tell. One afternoon he had a strange congregation in that little chapel. There were one hundred and forty-six native converts and twenty-one Europeans. These were made up of seven nationalities, British, American, French, Danish, Turkish, Swiss, and Norwegian. Their ship was from America and was bound for Hongkong with coal-oil.

They were amazed at seeing a pretty, neat chapel away in this wild, remote place, which they had always supposed was overrun by head-hunters, and indeed it was just that little chapel that had made the great change. These men now entered it and joined the natives in worshiping the true God, where, only a few years before, their blood would have stained the sands.

A Hoa told them something of the great Kai Bok-su and the struggles he had had with savages and other enemies, when he first came to this region. The visitors were very much interested and did not wonder that the name "Kai Bok-su" was held in such reverence. When they left, the captain presented the little chapel with a bell, a lamp, and a mirror which were on board his ship.

The long months of separation were rolling around, when something happened that brought Kai Bok-su back to his island in great haste. Once more war swept over Formosa. This time the trouble was between China and Japan. The big Empire proved no match for the clever Japanese, and everywhere China was forced to give in.

One of the places which Japan set her affections on was Formosa. She must have the Beautiful Isle and have it at once. China was in no position to say no, so the Chinese envoy went on board a Japanese vessel and sailed toward Formosa. When in sight of its lovely mountains, without any ceremony he pointed to the land and said, "There it is, take it." And that was how Formosa became a province of Japan. At noon on May 26, 1895, the dragon flag of China was hauled down from Formosan forts and the banner of Japan was hoisted.

Of course this was not done without a

struggle. The Formosans themselves fought hard, and in the fight the Christians came in for times of trouble. So Kai Bok-su, hearing that his "valuables" were again in danger, set sail for Tamsui.

When he arrived the war was practically over, but everywhere were signs of strife. As soon as he was able, he took A Hoa and Koa Kau and visited the chapels all over the country. Everywhere were sights to make his heart very sad. The Japanese soldiers had used many of the chapels for military stables, and they were in a filthy state. At one place the native preacher was a prisoner, the Japanese believing him to be a spy. At another village the Christians sadly led their missionary out to a tea plantation and showed him the place where their beloved pastor had been shot by the Japanese soldiers. Mackay stood beside his grave, his heart heavy with sorrow.

But his courage never left him. The native Christians everywhere forgot their woes in the great joy of seeing him once more; and he joined them in a brave attempt to put things to rights once more. The Japanese paid for all damages done by their soldiers and in a short time the work was going on splendidly.

"We have no fear," wrote Dr. Mackay. "The King of kings is greater than Emperor or Mikado. He will rule and overrule all things."

His faith was rewarded, for when the troublous time was over, the government of Japan proved better than that of China, and on the whole the trial proved a blessing.

Oxford College had been closed while Dr. Mackay was away, and the girls' school had not been opened since the war commenced, for it was not safe for the girls and women to leave their homes during such disturbed times. But now both schools reopened, and again Kai Bok-su with his cane and his book and his crowd of students could be seen going up to the lecture halls, or away out on the Formosan roads.

He had conquered so often, overcome such tremendous obstacles, and faced unflinchingly so many awful dangers for the sake of his converts, that it was no wonder that they adored him, their feeling amounting almost to worship. "Kai Bok-su says it must be so" was sufficient to compel any one in the north Formosa Church to do what was required. Surely never before was a man so wonderfully rewarded in this life. He had given up all he possessed for the glory of his Master and he had his full compensation.

A few happy years sped round. The time for him to go back home again was drawing near when there came the first hint that he might soon be called on a longer furlough than he would have in Canada.

At first, when the dread suspicion began to be whispered in the halls of Oxford College and in the chapel gatherings throughout the country, people refused to believe it. Kai Bok-su ill? No, no, it was only the malaria, and he always arose from that and went about again. It could not be serious.

But in spite of the fact that loving hearts refused to accept it, there was no use denying the sad fact. There was something wrong with Kai Bok-su. For months his voice had been growing weaker, the doctors had examined his throat, and attended him, but it was all of no use. At last he could not speak at all, but wrote his words on a slate.

And everywhere in north Formosa, converts and students and preachers watched and waited and prayed most fervently that he might soon recover. Those who lived in Tamsui whispered to each other in tones of dread, as they watched him come and go with slower steps than they had been accustomed to see.

"He will be well next month," they would say hopefully, or, "He will look like himself when the rains dry." But little by little the conviction grew that the beloved missionary was seriously ill, and a great gloom settled all over north Formosa. There was a little gleam of joy when the doctor in Tamsui advised him finally to go to Hongkong and see a specialist. He went, leaving many loving hearts waiting anxiously between hope and fear to hear what the doctors would say. And prayers went up night and day from those who loved him. From the heart-broken wife in the lonely house on the bluff to the farthest-off convert on the Ki-lai plain, every Christian on the island, even those in the south Formosa mission, prayed that the useful life might be spared.

But God had other and greater plans for Kai Bok-su. He came back from Hong-kong, and the first look at his pale face told the dreaded truth. The shadow of death lay on it.

Those were heart-breaking days in north Formosa. From all sides came such messages of devotion that it seemed as if the passionate love of his followers must hold him back. But a stronger love was calling him on. And one bright June day, in 1901, when the green mountainsides, the blue rivers, and the waving rice-fields of Formosa lay smiling in the sun, Kai Bok-su heard once more that call that had brought him so far from home. Once more he obeyed, and he opened his eyes on a new glory greater than any of which he had ever dreamed. The task had been a hard one. The "big stone" had been stubborn, but it had been broken, and not long after the noontide of his life the tired worker was called home.

They laid his poor, worn body up on the hill above the river, beside the bodies of the Christians he had loved so well. And the soft Formosan grass grew over his grave, the winds roared about it, and the river and the sea sang his requiem.

Gallant Kai Bok-su! As he rests up there on his wind-swept height, there are hearts in the valleys and on the plains of his beloved Formosa and in his far-off native land that are aching for him. And sometimes to these last comes the question "Was it well?" Was it well that he should wear out that splendid life in such desperate toil among heathen that hated and reviled him? And from every part of north Formosa, sounding on the wind, comes many an answer.

Up from the damp rice-fields, where the farmer goes to and fro in the gray dawn, arises a song:

> I'm not ashamed to own my Lord,
> Or to defend his cause.

Far away on the mountainside, the once savage mother draws her little one to her and teaches him, not the old lesson of bloodshed, but the older one of love and kindness, and together they croon:

> Jesus loves me, this I know,
> For the Bible tells me so.

And up from scores of chapels dotting the land, comes the sound of the old, old story of Jesus and his love, preached by native Formosans, and from the thousand tongues of their congregations soars upward the Psalm:

> All people that on earth do dwell,
> Sing to the Lord with cheerful voice!

These all unite in one great harmony, replying, "It is well!"

But is it well with the work? What of his Beautiful Island, now that Kai Bok-su has left for a greater work in a more beautiful land? Yes, it is well also with Formosa. The work goes on.

There are two thousand, one hundred members now in the four organized congregations, and over fifty mission stations and outstations. But better still there are in addition twenty-two hundred who have forsaken their idols and are being trained to become church-members. The Formosa Church out of its poverty gives liberally too. In 1911 they contributed more than thirty-five hundred dollars to Christian work. "Every year," writes Mr. Jack, "a special collection is taken by the Church for the work among the Ami—the aborigines of the Ki-lai plain." This is the foreign mission of the north Formosa Church.

A Hoa lately followed his pastor to the home above, but many others remain. Mr. Gauld and his family are still there, in the front of the battle, and with him is a fine corps of soldiers, comprising fifty-nine native and several Canadian missionaries, including the Rev. Dr. J. Y. Ferguson and his wife, the Rev. Milton Jack and Mrs. Jack, the Rev. and Mrs. Duncan MacLeod, Miss J. M. Kinney, Miss Hannah Connell, Miss

Mabel G. Clazie, and Miss Lily Adair. Miss Isabelle J. Elliott, a graduate nurse, and deaconess, will join the staff shortly, and a few others will be sent when secured, in order that the force may be sufficient to evangelize the million people in north Formosa.

Mrs. Mackay and her two daughters, Helen and Mary, the latter having married native preachers, Koa Kau and Tan He, are keeping up the work that husband and father left. A new hospital is being built under Dr. Ferguson, and plans are on foot for new school and college buildings.

And the latest arrived missionary? What of him? Why his name is George Mackay, and he has just sailed from Canada as the first Mackay sailed forty-one years earlier. He has been nine years in Canada and the United States, at school and college, and now with his Canadian wife, has gone back to his native land. Yes, Kai Bok-su's son has gone out to carry on his father's work, and Formosa has welcomed him as no other missionary has been welcomed since Kai Bok-su's day.

But these are not all. From far across the sea, in the land where Kai Bok-su lived his boyhood days, comes a voice. It is the echo from the hearts of other boys, who have read his noble life. And their answer is, "We too will go out, as he went, and fight and win!"

CHAPTER XIV.

ELEVEN YEARS LATER.

THE year of Jubilee has come. The Church in North Formosa is now half a century old. From the day of small things the Christian cause in "The Island Beautiful"* has grown to gratifying dimensions. The preceding chapter gives some idea of the development which had been attained in 1912.

What a contrast between the early days of the "black-bearded barbarian" and now! Then MacKay's life was often in peril, today the missionary is highly esteemed. No longer is the missionary suspected; he is respected. He is now regarded as their best friend and even the heathen no longer call him "foreign devil."

Geo. W. MacKay, son of Kai Bok-su, is now translating Christian books into the Chinese language. One of the greatest needs of Christian people in a non-Chris-

---

*"The Island Beautiful," the story of fifty years in North Formosa by Duncan MacLeod, is a new book being read and studied throughout the Presbyterian Church in Canada

tain land is good literature, for of good reading there is a very meagre quantity indeed. Mr. MacKay is equipped for this necessary work because Chinese is as much his mother tongue as English. He teaches in the Theological College also, where there are at present seventeen students preparing for the ministry. Mrs. MacKay continues her helpful service to the mission and the church, giving many hours weekly to teaching.

For the Tamsui Middle School for boys commodious quarters and adequate equipment are being erected under Mr. Dowie's trained eye and within sight of the grave of our hero, the pioneer of the mission. Thanks to the Peace Thankoffering Fund which the Canadian Church subscribed in 1920, many new buildings, sorely needed, were made possible in lands where Canadian missionaries are working. Over one hundred boys are now being educated in the old dilapidated Oxford College. Most of the boys are not Christian when they enter, but nearly all are Christians when they leave. In fact the Middle School is the chief recruiting ground for the Theological College. The graduating class of nine in 1919 were all Christians and seven entered upon training to fit them as ministers of the gospel while the other two decided to study for Christian medical service.

The Theological College, too, has a new building which it is hoped will be large enough for a long time, though the growth of the Church may be such as will necessitate its enlargement.

Dr. Gauld (for his alma mater, Knox College, Toronto, honored him with the degree of D.D. in 1923) is still the Principal of the Theological College, and Rev. W. G. and Mrs. Coates have been sent to Formosa in order to help in the training of leaders for the Church.

The Tamsui Girls' School, under Miss Kinney and Miss Connell, is enlarging its usefulness year by year. Upwards of one hundred girls are given a Christian education. Parents are realizing the importance of sending their daughters as well as their sons to school.

But how much more might have been done if the Church in Canada had sent more men and women like those who have been or are now there? Repeatedly the call came from the hard-pressed band that more men and women be sent, but in vain, for even to-day there are only twenty all told in North Formosa. Only twenty at the close of fifty years! The wonder is that so much has been accomplished with so few missionaries. Surely there is no need to do more than state the requirements in "Canadians wanted" in order to ensure response from young men and women who long for the best investment of their lives!

Here is the list as sent to the Home Church by the Council of Missionaries:

MEN: Eight ministers, three doctors, three high school teachers, one chemist, one director of religious education and one business manager.

WOMEN: Five deaconesses, one doctor, three nurses, one music teacher and one household science teacher.

In this Jubilee Year of the North Formosa Church, will the Mother Church fail? Let the faith and the daring of the "black-bearded barbarian" stir the Church in Canada to answer the call and send reinforcements in these days of wide-open doors in "beautiful Formosa."

V.

W.

Y.

Z.

CPSIA information can be obtained at www.ICGtesting.com
Printed in the USA
LVOW01s1942190115

423463LV00020B/1095/P

9 781172 923298